T0120647

WHAT READERS ARE SAYING ABOUT "YOUR FAITH DETERMINES YOUR FUTURE":

This small book speaks volumes about the faith that God wants us to have and how to walk in it. Ps. Brendan is a man who writes not only from a sound grasp of scripture but also from conviction and experiences wrought in the furnace of faithfully serving our Lord. For he lives not in an ivory tower of biblical concepts but rather has walked in many challenging even life-threatening ministry situations. I love the fact he is vulnerable about his own faith, yet his personal stories inspire us to go further in our faith journey. I commend this book to all who seek to grow in their faith.

—Dr. Wilson Lim, PhD (Eng), president, Hope International Ministries (HIM) and founding pastor of Hope Church Brisbane

I have known Brendan Kirby for over twenty years since he first started the Hope Church in Adelaide in 1998. Brendan has been a friend and brother to me since 2012 after my dear wife passed away. From my interactions with Brendan over the years especially over our regular coffee catch-ups while I was still living in Adelaide, I found him to be a man of faith and integrity. And a man who loves the Word of God! Brendan took a big step of faith to leave his family, friends, and job in Melbourne to come to Adelaide to start the Hope Church. I am sure you will find this book to be insightful and practical as well for your faith journey!

—Ps. Andrew Evans (retired), senior pastor, Influencers Church, Paradise SA for thirty years; Australian National Chairman AOG for twenty years, founder of Family First (a political party in SA).

I have watched Pastor Brendan's journey of faith for more than fifteen years. This book reveals those principles of faith that God has revealed to him and what Pastor Brendan has learned from the Lord himself. I have ministered with Pastor Brendan in India and Africa, and I have seen him practicing what he preaches. He is genuine! This book is not just good learning, but it challenges you to do it!

—Ps. Simon Eng, elder, Hope International Ministries (HIM) and founding pastor of Hope Church Kuching.

My friend, Pastor Brendan Kirby, has written a practical and easy-to-read book that will bring the concept of faith to life! What I appreciate most is not just the biblically rooted ideas that he expounds on but also the personal stories he uses to make faith practical. I highly commend this book as a journey guide to anyone who is on this journey of faith.

—Ps. Benny Ho, senior pastor, Faith Community Church, founder, Arrows College, and leader of D-Net Network of Churches.

Few topics are as misunderstood as the subject of faith. Dr. Kirby's helpful book shines a light on this topic in a way that is scriptural, practical, and well reasoned. It is at once readable and easy to digest. Dr. Kirby unpacks the subject of faith from the scriptures with the logical mind of a physicist and laces it with faith-inspiring illustrations from personal experience that helps move the reader into faith. The greatest of electrical gadgets in our hands are useless until we can find the plug and get it connected to the source of power. In this regard, Dr. Kirby helps us to see how faith—that invisible spiritual plug—looks like and how it should be plugged into the source of power so that the potential power in God's promises may be released and realized in our lives. Then, we will indeed discover that "Our faith determines our future." This book is written by a scientist who has a passion for scripture, and is most certainly worthy of a read!

—Ps. Chris Liew, pastor, New Life Christian Community, Klemzig, South Australia

This is a "faith-encouragement" book that has come just at the right time for younger and older Christians alike in these end times when not only the love of many is waxing cold but also their faith is nose-diving!

Step by step, Pastor Brendan shows us what faith is and how to develop and grow it to robustness through God's Word applied to our daily endeavors.

Pastor Brendan, using examples from his personal life situations as well as biblical and contemporary heroes has in this book sought for us to develop such faith in God that remains steadfast and unflinching come rain, come sunshine. He shows us that though our faith may wobble initially, once we refuse to give up, God will help us become steady, trusting Him all the way, thereby reaping the fruit of our faith, i.e., accessing everything (all) that God has provided for us through Christ. So much wholesome teaching has been compressed into this book that would inspire any Christian at any stage of his or her faith journey. Hence, I have no hesitation in recommending it to the reading public. Thank you, Pastor Brendan, for this impactful book. More grace for greater exploits in Jesus's name, amen.

—Ps, Jane and Ps, Abraham Haastrup, overseers of Redeemed Christian Church of God (RCCG) Australia and South Pacific

I do appreciate the hard work, passion, and services Ps. Kirby exhibits to constantly reduce the kingdom of darkness and increase the kingdom of God. The subject of faith cannot be overstated for its importance to the believers in Christ, for without faith, our work with the Lord is questionable. Dr. Brendan has exposed the secret and power of having faith as a basic requirement to do the work of the kingdom of God. By faith, Dr. Brendan left Australia for Liberia without knowing who he was coming to, what people he was going to meet, what their cultural beliefs were, etc. Yet he counted his life nothing for the gospel of Jesus Christ, and by faith, he arrived in an unknown continent of Africa where he demonstrated his faith in the Lord. So his book *Your Faith Determines Your Future* will encourage you to explore your mind and develop your faith for the kingdom's purpose. Thanks, Ps. Brendan, for this faith lesson that will be a blessing to all the readers thereof.

—Rev. Sonny S. Brown, founder of Hope Church (HIM) Gbarnga, Liberia, West Africa, apostle, church planter, and overseer, HIM West Africa.

Paul writes to the Corinthians (2 Corinthians 5:7) to walk by faith and not by sight. Ps. Brendan outlines what this walk by faith looks like, the factors that will help you to have a successful walk, and the pitfalls that will trip you up. I encourage you to read this material so that you may have a faith walk that endures to the end.

—Rev. Dr. John Lucas, founder and president of Walking Free Renewing Ministries.

I have known Ps. Brendan Kirby for three years and have found him to be one who walks the walk when it comes to operating in the faith realm. His book not only gives us a foundation for operating in healing; it also has testimonies of his experiences as he has stepped out in faith whether it be in his local church in Adelaide or the mission fields of Africa and India.

—Rod Winter, national vice chairman, Full Gospel Business Australia (FGBA).

The intention of Pastor Brendan Kirby's brilliant book was to "equip and assist our brothers and sisters to grow and become great people for God and to play key roles in the extension of His kingdom!" With a careful blend of raw testimony, vulnerability, humor, distilled wisdom, and practical achievable advice following each chapter, I am confident that Brendan will succeed in his aim. Brendan and his inspirational wife, Helen, live and model this empowering message. I have personally witnessed their generosity of heart, sincerity, humility, and the exceptional quality of the sons and daughters they have raised. There is treasure in this book for everyone from the zealous young Christian who wants to lift faith's equivalent of 100kg to the veteran who needs a fresh perspective on the currency of heaven—faith.

—Mark Mudri, region leader South Australia/Northern Territory/Western Australia, Bible Society Australia.

Your Faith Determines Your Future!

Lifting the limits off your life

Dr. Brendan Kirby

WESTBOW
PRESS®
A DIVISION OF THOMAS NELSON
& ZONDERVAN

WestBow Press books may be ordered through booksellers or by contacting:

WestBow Press
A Division of Thomas Nelson & Zondervan
1663 Liberty Drive
Bloomington, IN 47403
www.westbowpress.com
844-714-3454

Scripture taken from the New King James Version®. Copyright © 1982 by Thomas Nelson. Used by permission. All rights reserved.

ISBN: 978-1-6642-3878-7 (sc)
ISBN: 978-1-6642-3879-4 (hc)
ISBN: 978-1-6642-3877-0 (e)

Library of Congress Control Number: 2021913069

Print information available on the last page.

WestBow Press rev. date: 07/24/2021

Hope Church
53 Fourth Avenue, Klemzig, Adelaide
SA 5070, Australia.
Webpage: www.hopeadelaide.com
YouTube Channel: @hopechurchadelaide
Email: info@hopeadelaide.com
Twitter: @drbrendankirby

MISSIONS SUPPORT INFORMATION

Profits from book sales shall be sent directly to pastors in India and Africa who are planting and building many churches with thousands of church members with so many needs and emergency requirements. If you would like to make a donation, see bank details below.

Account Name: Hope Missions Account
Account #118 373 340
BSB #105 056
SWIFT/BIC CODE for overseas transfers: SGBLAU2S
For USA transfers: Routing # 021 000 021
Bank SA, 87 John St, Salisbury, SA 5108, Australia
Receipts for use of missions gifts can be provided upon request.

CONTENTS

Missions Support Information.. vii

Introduction.. ix

Chapter 1   What Is Faith? 1

Chapter 2   Our Faith Can Grow.. 13

Chapter 3   No Doubt about It... 23

Chapter 4   Overcoming Self-Doubt.................................... 33

Chapter 5   Your Faith Determines Your Future............... 41

Chapter 6   Inheriting the Promises and Overcoming the
             Seven Enemies of Our Faith 53

Chapter 7   Faith to Overcome Failures............................... 63

Chapter 8   How to Overcome Negative Feelings 73

Epilogue... 85

Acknowledgments... 87

Not that we have dominion over your faith, but are fellow
workers for your joy; for **by faith you stand**.

—2 Corinthians 1:24

INTRODUCTION

If you will not **believe**, surely you shall not be **established**.
—Isaiah 7:9

"Your faith determines your future" is a bold statement that challenges us to consider the extent of its truth and to reflect on the emphasis we place on faith in our lives. Are we actively pursuing a stronger faith that will impact the world around us, or are we content with a routine or a ritual that makes our lives comfortable but perhaps lacks the impact it might otherwise have?

The promises of God to those who have faith and do not doubt are incredible, and we desperately need to unlock the secrets of faith as we press on as ambassadors for the kingdom of God and colaborers in the building of His church in this world.

I wrote this book to encourage people to inherit all that God has for them in this world and in the world to come. God is so great and amazing that He has an awesome, detailed, and inspiring plan for each of us. But I find that some Christians struggle for different reasons to receive from God and then to serve Him.

The intention of this book is to motivate, inspire, and help equip and assist our brothers and sisters in the development of their faith and become great people for God and to play key roles in the extension of His kingdom.

To be effective, whatever is taught needs to be commensurate with scriptural principles (since the Word of God is immutable and God will watch over His word to perform it; Jer 1:12). Therefore, all the teaching is referenced diligently to the Bible. (Unless otherwise noted, scripture references are from the NKJV.)

The Great Commission is a daunting task, but with apostolic and prophetic power and authority, many networks of churches around the world today are doing a great job planting many churches, training pastors and leaders, and seeing many souls added to God's kingdom regularly.

The key to our personal growth, success in life, and a more effective ministry is our faith. God is not holding us back; our lack of faith is often the real problem.

I pray that we will all be able to take on the challenge that scripture gives to us to grow in faith, to slay our personal, spiritual Goliaths that intimidate us at one stage or another, and to receive the miraculous promises from heaven, amen.

Let us together look at some salient scriptures on faith and inspire one another to reach up to greater heights to reveal the glory of our great God and Savior, the Lord Jesus Christ.

Love,
Brendan Kirby
Hope Church, Adelaide
Member of Hope International Ministries (HIM)

CHAPTER 1
What Is Faith?

Believe in the Lord your God, and you shall be established;
believe His prophets, and you shall prosper.

—2 Chronicles 20:20

In 1984, I experienced a year of confusion and uncertainty about my future, and my motivation for my research project was severely waning. Finally in October, I made a big commitment to follow Jesus Christ in the Arts Lecture Theatre at the University of Melbourne in front of about forty fellow students of whom more than half were actively involved in mocking and deriding David Miles, the bold young speaker declaring the truth of the Word of God to us. It was probably the worst meeting I have ever attended. So many were mocking David. Cries such as "Rubbish!" "Go home!" "Don't believe it!" and "Boo!" rang through the theater.

One fourth-year physics student I recognized was slithering down the steps of the lecture theater like a snake and laughing in protest of the words being spoken. It was pandemonium. Almost everybody was talking during the message, and hardly anyone was listening—except me. Somehow, in the midst of this cacophony, David sensed to do an altar call for salvation—and it struck a deep chord of agreement in me. He asked me to stand up (I was seated at the back of the theater) and pray out loud this prayer of faith and repentance in front of my fellow students. There were three postgraduate students from the physics department sitting behind me, and they could not believe what they saw me do. This commitment changed my entire life and perspective. I was truly born again and became a new man—I sensed in the following days that my motives and feelings toward normal things were changing quickly.

That was the beginning of my journey of faith, which consisted of many tests and trials through each of which I learned more about the Lord's expectations about my trust in Him and about my faith in His purposes to always work out for the best if I continued to obey and trust in Him (Rom. 8:28).

Abraham—The Man of Faith

Abraham was commended by God as our father of faith, our father of circumcision, the father of many nations, and the father of us all (Rom. 4). Abraham had no police force, no local church support, and no missionary agency encouraging him when King Chedorlaomer kidnapped his nephew with four other kings who had just ravaged the countryside (Gen. 14). Abraham faced his struggles and difficulties of living in a foreign land with a different culture and behavior set (including the stigma of not having any children) by faith in the God who had called him (Gen. 15).

His faith was his bedrock, his foundation for living. He had decided when he was young to honor God and put Him first, and by doing so, he attracted God's attention so that God called him to leave Ur of the Chaldeans to "a land that I will show you" (Gen. 12:1). Abraham's obedience and faith became an example for all of us (Heb. 11:8). Consequently, the Lord calls us to "look to the rock from which you were hewn, and the hole from which we were dug" (Isa. 52:1). Abraham is then our example of a man of faith. This faith is outlined in Romans 4 beginning with Abraham's faith in God, which was reckoned to him as right standing before God (Gen. 15:6). Then it culminates with his growing faith in the following verses, where he was able to receive the promise of God.

> Who, contrary to hope, in hope believed, so that he became the father of many nations, according to what was spoken, "So shall your descendants be." And not being weak in faith, he did not consider his own body, already dead (since he was about a hundred years old), and

the deadness of Sarah's womb. He did not waver at the promise of God through unbelief, but was strengthened in faith, giving glory to God, and being fully convinced that what He had promised He was also able to perform. And therefore "it was accounted to him for righteousness." (Rom. 4:18–22)

The scripture here states that Abraham was not weak in faith (hence, it is possible to be weak in our faith) and that he was strengthened in faith (so it is possible to grow stronger in our faith). If we are to "look to the rock from which we were hewn," it is crucial for us to learn to walk by faith and to please the Lord as Abraham did. We begin with some definitions.

How Can I Begin to Believe?

Faith is a choice. We can choose to believe a lot of things in our normal lives that are true and untrue (Jer. 40:16). We believe in electricity; we cannot see electrons, but we know they exist because of their effect. We know gravity exists through obvious consequences, but do we all believe in a warped space-time manifold? Sometimes, we can make choices based on personal moral preferences rather than an honest pursuit of truth or integrity; such is the deceitfulness of the human heart (Jer. 17:9). For example, numerous people will reject Jesus Christ based on a distorted perception of either the church or of a holy lifestyle without seeking the historical evidence for the life and claims of Jesus Christ (Acts 26:24).

Some choose to believe that the earth is flat despite clear evidence to the contrary—This is the amazing power of choice (1 Kings 18:21). We can choose to believe the truth based on the evidence available (Josh. 24:15), or we can reject the evidence and believe what is actually not true (Deut. 30:19). The Bible calls this unbelief—where we choose to believe the opposite of what is either clearly true or against what God says (Heb. 3:12–13, 18–19).

God desires for the people He loves to inquire after the truth (John 3:21), seek for greater significance, meaning, and purpose (Isa. 55:6), and decide to believe the promises of eternal life given to us through His Son, the Lord Jesus Christ (John 6:40, 3:3). This is the beginning or germination of the spiritual-based reality of our faith journey (Mark 11:22).

What Is Faith?

Faith is a spiritual substance—It has evidence of its existence. It is not an intellectual assent or a set of doctrinal statements.

> Now faith is the *substance* of things hoped for, the *evidence*
> of things not seen. (Heb. 11:1; italics added)

Faith is believing the words of those we trust (Prov. 3:5–6). When we trust others, we believe what they tell us. If we do not believe them, we do not trust their word. God is not happy if we do not believe what He says because it implies that we do not trust Him, which is tantamount to saying He is untrustworthy. We should consider this carefully as there is no one more trustworthy than the Lord. We may misunderstand Him, but that does not cast aspersions on His trustworthiness. For example, Abraham trusted God so much that when asked to sacrifice the son he loved, he demonstrated unwavering trust and prompt obedience (Gen. 22:1). And Job also showed great trust in the Lord (Job 13:15). In Romans 4:20, we see that Abraham did not waver in doubt or unbelief; he made a decision to believe that the words spoken to him would come to pass.

Faith makes a decision to believe the Word of God and does not wait in uncertainty or doubt. Abraham did not allow his feelings or his circumstances to change his mind. He walked by faith and pleased God.

> But without faith it is impossible to please Him, for he
> who comes to God must believe that He is, and that He is
> a rewarder of those who diligently seek Him. (Heb. 11:6)

God expects and even commands us to have faith. Why is faith so important to the Lord?

> But let him ask in faith, with *no doubting*, for he who
> doubts is like a wave of the sea driven and tossed by the

wind. For let not that man suppose that he will receive anything from the Lord. (James 1:6, 7; italics added)

James tells us that if we doubt, we will not receive anything from God—we receive things from God because we believe He will do what He has promised to do. This can be a source of confusion for young Christians yet to receive answers to their prayers. Sometimes as young Christians, God gives us a lot of things seemingly without us even asking. But soon, we realize that answers to prayers do not come because we cry and wail but because we choose to believe in God's promises.

In Hebrews 11:6, the Lord went as far as to say that we could not please Him without faith. Wow. But what does that mean? We will look at this question in more detail in this book.

Abraham walked by faith and discovered that we were saved by faith (Gen. 15:6).

For by grace you have been saved through faith, and that not of yourselves; it is the gift of God, not of works, lest anyone should boast. (Eph. 2:8–9)

Michael Fackerell (2007) wrote that faith was *not* religion, or mental assent, or a way to manipulate God, or a positive desire, or an attitude of seeing is believing.

Religion and traditional ways of behavior do not generate faith in the heart. Many professing Christians believe mentally that the Bible is the Word of God, but the Bible does not teach that we believe in our minds; in contrast, the Bible tells us, "With the heart one believes" (Rom 10:9). Therefore, we need to learn how to differentiate between what we think in our minds and what we believe in our hearts. This is a journey of self-awareness and testing ourselves.

Sometimes, people teach that faith is just making up our minds about what we want and asking for it based on Mark 11:24, but that borders on new age scripting where we are our own gods and determine our own destinies. We see in 1 John 5:14–15 that it is not that simple. Self-centered people and even some well-meaning Christians do not always know what is best to ask for. So God wants us to align ourselves with His will and to ask according to it. Romans 8:26–27 indicates that the Spirit makes intercession for the saints "according to the will of God."

It is God's will that we are pursuing, not our own desires. We do not choose to have faith in what we want; we choose to have faith in what God has clearly promised us (Rom. 4:21).

Faith is not hope, but hope strengthens and informs our faith. We all hope that our loved ones with cancer will recover, but hope will not bring the healing. My emergency does not generate faith in my heart. I need to train myself to believe in my heart for a miracle a long time before the pressure hits. In fact, as we discuss in a later chapter, fear and anxiety rather than faith will often hit us when a close family member is diagnosed with cancer. This is another major source of confusion for unsuspecting believers. Remember that God is not the author of confusion but of peace, so as we increase in self-awareness, we can observe our own levels of confusion (1 Cor. 14:33).

These points help to set a stage to understand clearly what faith is not and thereby provide an opportunity for us to know what faith actually is. For example, if I have anxiety, fear, or confusion operating in my heart, there will not be much faith present; I can't have both.

How Do I Know if I Have Faith?

God will answer our prayers. We know we have faith when we have received answers to our prayers and requests of God.

Some people assert that they have a strong faith and speak fluently about the scriptures, but then they wonder why their expectations were not met. Because of their false confidence, they become confused or worse deceived as to why these expectations were not met. We need to humble ourselves and recognize that we are not always paragons of faith even if sometimes we are. So we need to test ourselves to see if we are in the faith.

After a crusade in Kampala, Uganda, in 2016, I prayed for a delightful three-year-old girl who was deaf. Here was a perfect platform for a miracle … But nothing happened. After a frustrating ten minutes of fairly intense and heartfelt prayer, I committed her and her parents to the Lord.

Why was there no miracle? I can't say that the girl had a big sin problem! I have to look in the mirror and admit that perhaps my faith was not strong enough that day (Mark 9:28–29). I do know that my preparation for those crusade meetings was not exemplary. Who knows if she was healed later on? Probably not. I think the parents would have made contact with us if she had been. Yet in India and Africa, we have seen numerous deaf ears healed, and on one occasion in India a blind lady seeing, but on different days and with better preparation (fasting and prayer) well beforehand.

> So Jesus answered and said to them, "Have faith in God. For assuredly, I say to you, whoever says to this mountain, 'Be removed and be cast into the sea,' and **does not doubt** in his heart, but believes that those things he says will be done, he will have whatever he says. Therefore I say to you, whatever things you ask when you pray, believe that you receive them, and you will have them." (Mark 11:22–24)

Jesus made this amazing promise to all of us—If we have faith (and trust in the promises of God) and do not doubt, we will see great miracles. How awesome is that? Yet some of us give up after having tried to walk by faith and not having seen the miracle. We must persevere in our walk of faith, amen!

An analogy of going to a gym for the first time and attempting to bench press 100kg is relevant. Any regular gym goer will confidently assert that it will take years to become strong enough to lift that weight. It takes many years of faithful dedication to training regularly and a consistent healthy diet to build the appropriate muscle base to support such weight. The mistake we sometimes make as Christians is that we enter our spiritual gym and expect the miracle (to lift 100kg) without having done the preparation. The requisite preparation is in the heart; hence, the self-analysis of our own heart attitudes and motives is critical in the development of our faith.

> Beloved, **if our heart does not condemn us**, we have confidence toward God. And whatever we ask we receive

from Him, because we keep His commandments and do those things that are pleasing in His sight. (1 John 3:21–22)

I know I have faith when my heart does not condemn me. I have confidence before the Lord. If I am obeying all His commandments and doing the things that are pleasing to Him, I will see miracles, amen.

I was in India in 2016 at a crusade with more than two hundred people present. Everyone was clearly expecting a miracle. There were many sick and afflicted there. At the end of the preaching, a good number gave their hearts to the Lord Jesus Christ, for which we were very grateful. But we also saw the power of the Spirit operating. What characterized that meeting was that I had a lot of peace and no doubt that we would see God move. In one case, a man whose shoulder had been damaged in a car accident some five months previously was really shocked when he could move his arm up and down with no pain immediately after prayer. The expression on his face was a mixture of joy and surprise—wonderful to see!

Test Yourself: Are You in the Faith or Not?

Examine yourselves as to whether you are in the faith. Test yourselves. Do you not know yourselves, that Jesus Christ is in you?—unless indeed you are disqualified. (2 Cor. 13:5)

The scripture exhorts us to examine ourselves. Self-awareness is a practice we cannot afford to neglect. "Why did I just say that? What was motivating me? Why did I get so angry so quickly? What values am I adhering to that I responded that way under pressure?" These are the types of questions we need to be continually asking ourselves to understand the state of our hearts.

A good practice is to write out the values we should be living by and assess our words, thoughts, and behaviors against those values. Our thoughts are just as important as our words when we seek to generate more faith in our hearts since our thoughts reflect our inner motives (1 Cor. 4:5; Pss. 19:14, 139, 23, 24).

Doubt (James 1:6–7), fear (2 Tim. 1:7), confusion (1 Cor. 14:33), and anxiety (Phil. 4:6) are not the fruit of faith. If we show these symptoms and attitudes, it indicates that we have little faith. We must consistently look for these weeds of doubt, fear, confusion, and anxiety that spring up in our hearts all too easily and pray through their root cause to get back to the place of faith and trust in the Lord. Insecurity and a lack of acceptance can often be the causes of these spiritual weaknesses. These weaknesses can drive us toward all sorts of carnal motivations such as man's approval, selfish ambition, and attention-seeking behavior.

Feckerell stated, "Faith is a rest. It is compatible with inner peace. It is not trying to believe."

Scratched on the walls of one of the Nazi prison camps of World War II were the words "I believe in the sun even when it does not shine. I believe in love even when it is not expressed. And I believe in God even when He is silent" (Engler 2002).

Faith proves itself by its good deeds. Faith produces the fruit of the Spirit—love, joy, peace, goodness, kindness, patience, self-control, long-suffering, and gentleness (Gal. 5:22–23).

> What does it profit, my brethren, if someone says he has faith but does not have works? Can faith save him? If a brother or sister is naked and destitute of daily food, and one of you says to them, "Depart in peace, be warmed and filled," but you do not give them the things which are needed for the body, what does it profit? **Thus also faith by itself, if it does not have works, is dead** ... For as the body without the spirit is dead, so faith without works is dead also. (James 2:14–17, 26)

Faith Is the Currency of Heaven—Don't Give Up!

The great faith preacher and evangelist to Africa, Reinhard Bonnke, wrote in one of his many books on faith years ago, "No money = no buy!" He stated that our faith is the currency of heaven (Bonnke 2005). A key concept that some people stumble over is that they keep thinking faith is in the mind, and that when they're ever in trouble, they can just cry out and call on the Lord and it will all be fine. Yes, sometimes a last minute desperate reaching out to God can reap positive results – but in the midst of fear and anxiety I believe it is an unwise practice.

It would be like not exercising for twenty years until the doctor says we are about to have a heart attack and then engaging in frenzied exercising to prevent it. Better late than never, for sure; but risky. Why do we expect to bulk up our faith right when we need it to? If we cannot handle our spiritual emergencies, we blame the Lord. This is a sad misconception that weakens and even derails some in their faith walks.

My emergency does not produce faith; faith comes from the Word of God. Romans 10:17 reads, "So then faith comes by hearing, and hearing by the word of God."

Faith is like a cheque from God that we can cash; He is trustworthy, and He always has resources to back His promises. But if I do not practice walking by faith and then suddenly I get a serious disease, God may not heal me just because I have a sudden need. I still have to walk by faith. Let us not give up on our faith. We need to persevere! We all get discouraged at times (Heb. 10:35–36) even when we are close to our breakthrough, but we must keep going. We need to build up the level of cash in the bank (symbolically speaking) so our faith "cheque" will not bounce.

Florence Chadwick learned this lesson the hard way. After attempting what no woman had ever achieved in 1952—to swim across the Catalina Channel—and giving up within only thirty minutes of land due to exhaustion and the thick fog, Chadwick exclaimed, "Look, I'm not excusing myself, but if I could have seen land, I know I could have made it!" The fog had made her unable to see her goal, and it had felt to her like she was getting nowhere. Two months later, she tried again. The fog was just as dense, but that time, she made it (Chadwick).

Like Chadwick, we can continue in our battle to fulfill God's calling on our lives when engulfed with confusion or fog as long as we believe that the goal and the vision are still viable. We can do it because God is with us. "He heeded their prayer, because they put their trust in Him" (1 Chron. 5:20).

The example of Ida Lewis is also an inspiration as she proved faithful to her calling over many years as a lighthouse operator who saved over twenty-five men from drowning in the sea with her own hands (Patrick 2005). We too can fulfill our calling!

Conclusion

Faith pleases God. God draws near to us when we draw near to Him and are obedient and have faith. So having a strong, unshakeable faith is very important. Without faith, it is impossible to please the Lord. We need to learn to walk by faith, to practice so that we can get better each day. Faith is the key to unlocking our future. With faith, all things are possible, but without faith, we achieve very little for the Lord.

How Do I Respond?

Some of us have given up on walking by faith as if it does not work. We have begun to doubt whether God will work on our behalf. But faith does work. Today, let us choose again to believe that God can do it and to cultivate our faith.

Some of us need to forgive today.

> And whenever you stand praying, if you have anything against anyone, forgive him, that your Father in heaven may also forgive you your trespasses. But if you do not forgive, neither will your Father in heaven forgive your trespasses. (Mark 11:25–26)

Some of us need to choose not to doubt any longer and to start walking by faith. Make up your mind. Double-minded people are those who have not yet decided what they really value or what they desire to see fulfilled in their lives. (Read R. C. Sproul's book.)

Today, some of us need to commit our lives to Jesus Christ for the first time. He is the Son of God, and He loves us so much that He died for us to pay the penalty for our wrongdoings.

Chapter Summary

Faith is a choice.

Faith believes what God has promised.

Faith is a spiritual substance; it has evidence of its existence.

Faith is believing the words of someone you trust.

Faith makes a decision to believe the Word of God and does not wait in uncertainty or doubt.

Abraham walked by faith and discovered that we were saved by faith.

Faith is not hope, but hope strengthens and informs our faith.

Jesus promised us that if we had faith (and trusted in the promises of God) and did not doubt, we would see great miracles.

My emergency does not produce faith. Faith comes from the Word of God.

Faith produces the fruit of the Spirit—love, joy, peace, goodness, kindness, patience, self-control, long-suffering, and gentleness.

References

Michael Fackerell. 2007. "Faith in God." https://godisforreal.wordpress. com/2011/04/26/what-is-faith/#more-138.

Mark Engler. 2002. https://www.sermoncentral.com/illustrations/ sermon-illustration-mark-engler-stories-endurance-9620.

Reinhard Bonnke. 1999. *Faith: The Link with God's Power. Sovereign World Ltd, Tonbridge, England. 345p.*

Tim Patrick. 2005. Re: Ida Lewis. https://www.sermoncentral.com/sermons/ god-is-light-tim-patrick-sermon-on-promises-of-god-84767?page=2.

Florence Chadwick. Biography. https://biography.yourdictionary.com/ florence-chadwick.

R. C. Sproul. 1993. "Addressing our Doubts Leads to Certainty."

CHAPTER 2
Our Faith Can Grow

Whoever **believes** will not act hastily.

—Isaiah 28:16

Two months after my conversion in late 1984 as a young Christian, I was thrown into a significant trial that would determine whether I would complete a PhD in physics. I had failed my fifth-year research report, an incredible failure that nobody in my department would forgive me for as "Nobody fails the fifth-year report!" But I listened to a preaching tape and learned that my faith was like a muscle and could grow stronger. That excited me, and I threw myself into my work in my sixth year in an attempt to redeem my broken reputation. This was my first major crisis through which I learned to pray and trust in God.

By the middle of 1985, my research supervisor, Dr George Legge, had passed my report, and I was officially enrolled in the PhD program. This had been a big battle of faith for me, and God had come through in victory in providing good progress in my research and its results. I was inspired to see what further challenges God would conquer in my life—by faith. There were some minor challenges in the ensuing couple of years, but I was making progress in my walk with the Lord.

Lord, Increase our Faith

It must have been incredibly inspiring for the apostles to travel with the Lord and see all the great miracles He was doing. A realization began to dawn on them—to do miracles like Jesus, they needed to grow in their faith. We read in Luke 17 how they came to the Lord wanting to grow in their faith.

> And the apostles said to the Lord, **"Increase our faith."** So the Lord said, "If you have faith as a mustard seed, you can say to this mulberry tree, 'Be pulled up by the roots and be planted in the sea,' and it would obey you. And which of you, having a servant plowing or tending sheep, will say to him when he has come in from the field, 'Come at once and sit down to eat'? But will he not rather say to him, 'Prepare something for my supper, and gird yourself and serve me till I have eaten and drunk, and afterward you will eat and drink'? Does he thank that servant because he did the things that were commanded him? I think not. So likewise you, when you have done all those things which you are commanded, say, **'We are unprofitable (or unworthy) servants.** We have done what was our duty to do.'" (Luke 17:5–10)

The key revelation we want to build on here is that our faith is not a stagnant, unchanging entity or a mere intellectual concept but a dynamic, changing state of the heart in its attitude toward God's promises.

Jesus' reply cast a vision for the great things that faith the size of a mustard seed could achieve and described the need for genuine character reform and change into an obedient servant; that was probably not the way to grow in faith the apostles were expecting. The character qualities of obedience, servanthood, and humility cannot be overlooked on our journey to increase in faith.

Why Do I Need to Have Faith?

> Now faith is the substance of things hoped for, the evidence of things not seen. (Heb. 11:1)

The writer of Hebrews exhorts us that faith is a substance. Clearly, he did not mean a physical, material substance; he was likely referring to a substance in the spiritual realm that could be measured or weighed. Jesus referred to faith having a size (that of a mustard seed) and an amount (little or great); this tends to confirm that our faith can be estimated in the spiritual realm for its strength and that its impact is felt in our experience here in space and time.

The Bible says we must exercise faith.

> But without faith it is impossible to please Him, for he who comes to God **must believe that He is**, and that He is a rewarder of those who diligently seek Him. (Heb. 11:6)

This is a strong encouragement to approach the Lord by faith with our requests; words such as *must* and *impossible* indicate that God takes this very seriously. So let us continue to get out of our boats of security and comfort, step into an uncertain world, and practice our faith.

Without faith, we cannot be saved.

> For by grace you have been **saved through faith**, and that not of yourselves; it is the gift of God, not of works, lest anyone should boast. (Eph. 2:8–9)

Sometimes, we think our salvation is assisted by our kindness or sincerity or by our good works. But Jesus made it very clear that He was the author of our salvation (Heb. 12:2), that He was the only way to the Father (John 14:6), and that as an unclean people, we could never please God (Hag. 2:14). This was emphasized by Paul when he wrote that if we could be saved any other way, then God had made a mistake having His only Son crucified for us (Gal. 2:21).

Note that an unclean person cannot come into God's presence (Lev. 22:3, 32; Heb. 10:19–20). We can be made holy only by that which is holy. No good work can make us holy; it is imparted to us by something already made holy or by someone who is holy. Hence, Isaiah's lament that he was unclean (Isa. 6:5) where this was taken away by the "coal from the altar" (Isa. 6:7).

Therefore, to be made holy and to gain access to the Father can occur only if we are cleansed by the blood of Jesus (1 John 1:9). Our salvation was completed by Jesus Christ; there is no other way we can be forgiven or made holy. This is what we believe by faith and thereby receive the gift of God (in Romans 5:15–18, the word *gift* appears six times in four verses), which is eternal life. Without this faith, we cannot be saved.

The same faith for salvation is applicable for miracles and for all the promises of God if we simply receive and "only believe" (Mark 5:36) what God has already achieved (1 Pet. 2:24) and what He wants to do through us for His glory (2 Cor. 1:20). It is not based on our virtue or ability but on our faith in God's Word that He will do great things through us (Jer. 33:3).

Faith is not in the mind but in the heart!

> If you confess with your mouth the Lord Jesus and **believe in your heart** that God has raised Him from the dead, you will be saved. For with **the heart one believes** unto righteousness, and with the mouth confession is made unto salvation. (Rom. 10:9–10)
>
> … that Christ may dwell in your hearts through faith … (Eph. 3:17)

This is where it is easy for us Christians exercising our faith to get confused. We have a conviction in our minds that God will give us a certain thing as an answer to prayer not knowing that it is an intellectual ascent that we are praying from—not out of faith in the heart confident that we are asking according to the will of God (1 John 5:14–15).

When I was in Sydney on a holiday in 1986, I decided that I would win a car raffle. I bought one ticket and walked around the car by faith and claimed that car for myself in the name of Jesus. I labeled it as my faith project and went away very self-confident. I thought it was interesting that this faith project failed. Along my journey of growing in faith, I had to reinterpret my understanding of faith and how it worked in accordance with this failure to receive my promise.

It takes training to learn to discern ourselves and what the difference is. But if we have self-will, anxiety, fear, doubt, or uncertainty operating while we pray, it is usually a prayer from our minds. When we pray from the heart of faith, we exhibit the fruit of faith. Faith comes from hearing the Word of God (Rom. 10:17), so that word needs to be from the Bible or I need to hear a word from the Holy Spirit to my heart. The fruit of such faith is confidence, certainty, peace, and joy.

Without faith, our prayers will not be answered.

> Then the disciples came to Jesus privately and said, "Why could we not cast it out?" So Jesus said to them, "Because of your unbelief (or little faith)." (Matt. 17:19–20)

Here, Jesus stated that the reason we didn't receive answers to prayer (at least sometimes) was because of our little faith (unbelief). In Luke 9:41, Jesus used the word *faithless*. How important it is for us to drive out with determination the unbelief that hides in our hearts and limits the power of our prayers. Jesus Christ, the Son of God, went as far as to say that human beings could attain a level of spiritual experience where "all things are possible" if we believed. Surely pursuing the secrets behind such revolutionary potential is a worthy endeavor.

> "And often he has thrown him both into the fire and into the water to destroy him. But if You can do anything, have compassion on us and help us." Jesus said to him, **"If you can believe, all things are possible to him who believes."** Immediately the father of the child cried out

and said with tears, "Lord, I believe; help my unbelief!" (Mark 9:22–24)

Therefore I say to you, whatever things you ask when you pray, **believe** that you receive them, and you will have them. (Mark 11:24)

And whatever things you ask in prayer, **believing**, you will receive. (Matt. 21:22)

Friends, let's press in by faith (Hos. 6:3; Phil. 3:14) and release a greater power of God's Spirit in this world, amen.

Without faith, we cannot please God.

But without faith **it is impossible to please Him**, for he who comes to God must believe that He is, and that He is a rewarder of those who diligently seek Him. (Heb. 11:6)

God was pleased with His Son before He had even begun His ministry (Matt. 3:17) because Jesus had been living and walking by faith in all that He did up till that time. He had been walking with the Father and did by faith only what He was shown to do by Him (John 4:34, 5:19, 6:38). The diligent exercise of faith, obedience, and continual seeking of God's will pleases Him.

Without faith, we will give up more easily.

Now the just shall live by faith; but if anyone draws back, My soul has no pleasure in him. But we are not of those who draw back to perdition, but of those who believe to the saving of the soul. (Heb 10:38–39)

The enemy of our souls will wage war against our faith (Gal. 5:17; 1 Tim. 6:12) so that we fall back into doubt and fear. When we allow that to happen, we tend to give up more easily because fear and doubt see the magnitude of the problem and the impossibilities all too often.

We convince ourselves that we cannot go on all the while God is waiting to empower us and lead us to victory.

Our Faith Can Grow
Bukavu Church Building Raid

One morning in June 2016, about thirty Congolese government soldiers came to the church building in Nyawera, Bukavu. These soldiers were above the local police; they could actually kill people with impunity. They blocked off both entrances to the church, and some jumped over the high fence around the church office premises and went into the office where Mapya was praying. Some pointed guns at him and commanded him not to move while other soldiers thoroughly searched the entire building for a cache of guns that Mapya was allegedly selling according to a word spoken to the chief soldier by someone who wanted to malign the church.

They said to Mapya, "You move and we'll shoot you. We've come to kill you. You're selling guns!" Mapya said it wasn't true, that they had been misled, but the soldiers refused to listen. Mapya said to the soldiers pointing their guns at him, "You need Jesus! I am ready to die. I will go to heaven and I will be happy, but you need Jesus! Without Jesus, there is hell." Mapya rang some of his senior pastors and said, "Some soldiers are here. They might kill me. Please look after my family and the ministry for me."

Eventually, the soldiers completed their search, and the chief apologized to Mapya and told him, "You are a true man of God. We trust you now. Please pray for us to receive Jesus!"

While he was relating this story to me, Mapya said, "We must be ready to die every day for Jesus!" Mapya's stature as a man was hidden by his love for God and humility before men.

Ps. Mapya had begun his ministry in 1998 with just his family after giving up his job as a school teacher. After twenty-plus years of hard work and walking for days up and down mountainous terrain to plant churches and preach the gospel among the Congolese people, he now leads over a hundred churches and conducts regular pastors' training, which some pastors walk for two days (sometimes in the rain) and sleep by the side of the road to attend. Ps. Mapya's faith has grown to the level that he is quite prepared to live or die for the gospel and his love for Jesus. We too can apply ourselves and see our faith grow and overcome inordinate odds and achieve great exploits for the Lord.

> The people who know their God will be strong and carry out great exploits. (Dan. 11:32)

The Word of God is our reference for all our doctrine, beliefs, and practices as followers of Jesus Christ. It is incumbent on us to know how the Bible describes the pathway to develop in this important area of faith that affects our lives. It is encouraging to see the scripture state that the men of old "out of weakness were made strong" (Heb. 11:34), that the apostles "grew bold" (Acts 13:46), and even the apostle Paul "grew all the more in strength," "took courage," and was "encouraged" by meeting with the saints in Rome (Acts 9:22, 28:15; Rom. 1:12).

This means that it is possible for weak people (like me) to grow in strength and courage and that our faith can become stronger. Hallelujah! This gives us confidence that the mountain we cannot move today will move in the near future if we set ourselves to pursue our faith in God. These following scriptures gives us hope that as our faith increases, we can begin to see greater moves of God in our lives.

> And the apostles said to the Lord, **"Increase our faith."** (Luke 17:5)

> We are bound to thank God always for you, brethren, as it is fitting, because **your faith grows exceedingly**, and the love of every one of you all abounds toward each other. (2 Thess. 1:3)

> … not boasting of things beyond measure, that is, in other men's labours, but having hope, that **as your faith is increased**, we shall be greatly enlarged by you in our sphere. (2 Cor. 10:15)

The way our faith grows is not always tangible or detectable by a cursory glance. As in Luke 17, it can be the slow development of a character base determined to honor God in every area of life.

Have Faith in Jesus Christ, the Son of God

In a world full of compromise, syncretism, and pluralism, we need to continually "contend earnestly" for our faith in the Lord Jesus Christ (Jude 3). He is our Savior, and He is our God, the Creator of the universe (John 1:1–3; Col. 1:15–16). If all else fails in this life, we must never let go of our grip on Jesus, the key to our eternal life.

> Jesus said to her, "I am the resurrection and the life. He who believes in Me, though he may die, he shall live. And whoever lives and believes in Me shall never die. Do you believe this?" (John 11:25–26)

As Josh McDowell so eloquently argued years ago, Jesus Christ was either the Lord He said He was, a liar who had deceived those who lived with Him for over three years, or a lunatic for saying what He said (McDowell 1980). These are the only logical options. He cannot be a prophet or a good teacher because a good man does not say, "If you have seen Me you have seen the Father!" (John 14:9) nor does a prophet say, "I am the Son of God" (John 10:33, 36) or "he who believes in Me I will give eternal life."

Conclusion

Today, let us hear the Word of God and believe it. Romans 10:17 reads, "So then faith comes by hearing, and hearing by the word of God."

Let us begin to practice what we know is right. Luke 17:5–10 tells us to serve by faith not looking for man's approval but believing that God is watching, amen!

How Do I Respond?

Friends, please give your heart to Jesus Christ if you have not already done so. He is our only confidence of eternal life. There is no one else. No one else has ever died for our wrongdoings and then risen from the dead to lead us to eternal life. Let us continue to hold fast to our confession of faith in Jesus no matter what trials get thrown at us; remember the martyrs of the early church described in *Foxe's Book of Martyrs*.

Chapter Summary

Our faith is a dynamic, changing state of the heart in its attitude toward God's promises.

Our faith can grow.

The Bible says we must exercise faith.

Without faith, we cannot be saved.

Without faith, our prayers will not be answered.

Faith is not in the mind but in the heart.

Without faith, we cannot please God.

Without faith, we will give up more easily.

Reference

Josh McDowell 1980. "More Than a Carpenter." https://www.goodreads. com/book/show/313631.More_Than_a_Carpenter.

CHAPTER 3
No Doubt about It

And since we have the same spirit of faith, according
to what is written, "I believed and therefore I spoke,"
we also believe and therefore speak.

—2 Corinthians 4:13

In 2008, I had pastors' training meetings in Bukavu, DRC, and a pastor from Thailand was to travel with me. Before I departed for this trip, our HIM president asked me to go to Pakistan to meet a pastor who was interested in our movement and to conduct some meetings for him. After successful meetings in Bukavu, where many pastors were blessed and numerous healings were reported, I was about to begin my journey to Islamabad. The Thai pastor who was with me tentatively asked me, "Do you really want to go to Pakistan?" I looked at him a little nervously and said "Yes," but I checked again in my heart with the Lord and asked if this was what He really wanted me to do. The response I felt was *If you go, go by faith. Do not doubt!* That was my ticket. I determined to go by faith, and I knew God would help me.

Upon my arrival in Islamabad on September 25, the Taliban blew up the Marriott Hotel leaving about a hundred dead and probably over a hundred injured. I heard the explosion while I was speaking at a small church meeting. As I grew nervous about my safety, the pastor in charge of the meetings leaned over and said to me, "Do not worry. They are targeting foreigners!" I was perplexed how that would help me not to worry.

The whole time in Pakistan was a test of faith against my own fears. I felt completely alone in a strange, dangerous context (alienation of Western Christians) where even a Pakistani on the plane flying into Islamabad had asked me, "Why are you, a Westerner, visiting my country when even I am afraid to visit my own country?" I knew I was taking a big risk with this trip. I had never met the people into whose hands I was placing my life. Understandably, I was nervous, but I kept praying and walking by faith as best I could. During my stay the pastor would at various times turn to me and say "Those men over there would attack and beat us if they knew we were Christians!"

The next test came when the pastor said we would move the two-night crusade meetings from Islamabad to Wazirabad because of the recent terrorist attack. Again, he told me not to worry, but that didn't help when after a three-hour journey, an armed guard got into the car with us and told me that they had stuck paper advertisements for the crusade meetings all over the city with my photo on them. It got only more stressful when as I began to speak at the crusade meeting to perhaps eight hundred people, I saw four armed guards at the four corners of the compound that had no roof. That was unsettling. Then after I preached and prayed for the sick and invited a number of people to give their hearts to the Lord, the pastor rushed over and said, "Quick! Follow me! We must leave now! Come, come!" Fear kept trying to grip me, but I kept resisting and pushing it back. I remained calm, and I trusted in God, but it was certainly a tough situation. Emotionally, I was quite drained by the time I was flying out of Islamabad and I was relieved and in tears that I was still alive. What a challenge of faith that was.

How important is our faith in God to us? What would we give up for the sake of our faith in the Lord Jesus Christ? Sometimes, it is easy to take our faith in God for granted. We are all too familiar with God's love and easily become complacent. But how important is our faith to us? Would we give up our houses, our careers, our dreams, or our precious desires? This is an important question to answer as we move into this chapter on doubt. There will come a time for all of us that our faith will be tested (though perhaps not as strongly as Abraham in Genesis 22:1) and we will be tempted to doubt and ask ourselves, *Is it really worth this sacrifice?*

How Important Is Our Faith?

I would like to put to you this key statement: "My faith in God and in His Word is the most important possession I can have in this world." Have a think about this statement as we move on (also refer to Rev. 2:10, 12:11).

While Jesus was revealing His glory to His leading three apostles on the mountaintop (Luke 9:29; Mark 9:3; Matt. 17:2), the other apostles were in the valley below unsuccessfully attempting to overcome a demon. Their doubts began to affect the father of the boy for whom they had been praying. Descending the mountain, Jesus was disappointed with His disciples' lack of faith (Matt. 17:17), and the father was struggling to believe his son could be helped. But Jesus spoke the word of faith (Mark 9:23): "All things are possible to he who believes!" The distressed father replied with tears, "Lord, I believe; help my unbelief!" (Mark 9:24).

We all find ourselves in situations like the father of the boy in Mark 9. We pray and fast for what we are sure is God's will, but nothing happens. The devil seems to gain the victory. Our faith gets weaker, not stronger. We begin to doubt God's promises of deliverance and blessing. (Some of us are even tempted to change our theology based on such experiences—"God did not want to heal.") But when Jesus enters the scene, we realize the true picture—We actually had little faith, and doubt got the better of us.

The Testing of Our Faith

God will test our faith to reveal its strength (Gen. 22:1; Job 23:10; Isa. 48:10) and to reveal areas that need extra work (James 1:2–4). The apostle Paul stated to the church in Thessalonica that they were "praying exceedingly that we may see your face and perfect *what is lacking in your faith*" (1 Thess. 3:10). Paul assumed here that our faith could be strengthened and that it had areas of lack or weakness that needed perfecting.

Likewise, Jesus prayed for Peter that his faith would not fail (during his upcoming test of loyalty to the Lord, which he failed when he denied the Lord three times) and that he would return to strengthen his brethren: "But I have prayed for you, **that your faith should not fail**; and when you have returned to Me, strengthen your brethren" (Luke 22:32). So clearly, our faith needs a lot of work to go to the next level. If the apostle Peter needed to be strengthened in his faith, so do we.

Jairus's faith was tested in Mark 5 while his daughter was dying back home, and as Jesus was on His way to heal her, a woman with an issue of blood interrupted Jesus. Then Jairus was told that his daughter had just died. How would we act in such a situation? Would we complain about the woman whose body was healed of her blood flow and caused a delay? Would we get angry?

> While He was still speaking, some came from the ruler of the synagogue's house who said, "Your daughter is dead. Why trouble the Teacher any further?" As soon as Jesus heard the word that was spoken, He said to the ruler of the synagogue, **"Do not be afraid; only believe."** (Mark 5:35–36)

The pivotal time here is when the messengers had just told Jairus that his daughter was dead and to give up and come home alone. How did Jairus respond? After the delay because of the woman's interruption, did he allow his irritation to weaken his faith? The life of his daughter was in the balance, but Jairus responded admirably; he looked to Jesus for reassurance, and Jesus replied, "Do not be afraid, only believe." Perhaps someday, our struggles between doubt and faith might result in someone else's life being radically impacted.

Our faith is tested when circumstances arise that enable doubt to attack us. Abraham, Peter, and Jairus were attacked with doubt at pivotal times, but each handled that attack differently. How will we handle the attack of doubt when it comes?

If our faith is our most precious possession in this world, "being much more precious than gold" (1 Pet. 1:7), whatever attacks it must be addressed ruthlessly and overcome relentlessly to keep doubt from becoming the biggest enemy in our lives.

Some of us are afraid of sin, and we are continually battling it; we think that it is our biggest enemy. But as stated in the next chapter, we are set free from sin (Rom. 6:18, 22), so if we are still struggling with sin, it can actually be a faith problem. Therefore, doubt can be the real problem behind a lot of sin (Rom. 14:23). We doubt the validity of God's good promises and then take things into our own hands just the way Eve did in Genesis 3. Once we question God's character and motives and doubt whether He really will do what is best for us, rebellion and pride gain a foothold and self-will sets in. Submission to God's will has been rejected because of the deadly seed of doubt.

The strength of our faith is revealed by what doubts and fears we are able to overcome.

How Did Jesus Move His Apostles Out of Doubt into Faith?

Jesus grew His apostles' faith by patiently applying tests and trials to their lives, exposing their heart attitudes, gently rebuking them at times, and by expecting them to change. Jesus patiently addressed their questions, solved their problems, and revealed His will to them so that they were well equipped to overcome the enemy later in their ministry. He gave them His Spirit as a helper (the *Parakletos*) to provide clarity of mind and a cogent understanding of spiritual things.

Below are some salient scriptures regarding the apostles' lack of faith to show us that this issue afflicts all human beings at least at some stage.

"Be merciful to those who doubt" (Jude 22 NIV). Sometimes, we are quick to judge those in the Bible who did not respond correctly immediately. We reassure ourselves and confidently assert that we would have done better. (Bathsheba would never have tempted us! From the comfort of our couch, some of us, myself included, overestimate our faith.) But even after having seen Jesus resurrected from the dead, some of the apostles He had chosen to lead His church still doubted. So this is not an ordinary problem if it afflicts our greatest apostles.

> When they saw Him, they worshiped Him; but **some doubted**. (Matt. 28:17)

> And when they heard that He was alive and had been seen by her, **they did not believe**. ... And they went and

told it to the rest, but **they did not believe them either**. (Mark 16:11, 13)

Later He appeared to the eleven as they sat at the table; and **He rebuked their unbelief and hardness of heart**, because they did not believe those who had seen Him after He had risen. (Mark 16:14)

And their words seemed to them like idle tales, and they **did not believe them**. (Luke 24:11)

Then He said to them, "O foolish ones, and **slow of heart to believe** in all that the prophets have spoken!" (Luke 24:25)

Moving from Doubt to Faith

Harrison (1945) wrote about the great missionary to China, Hudson Taylor, who was on a becalmed ship near New Guinea that was headed to crash on the reefs. The first officer doubted the benefit of prayer, but after fervent prayer, Taylor was convinced God would answer with sufficient wind to rescue their lives. Hudson wanted the corners of the mainsail to be let down, but the first officer balked until the breeze in the topsail picked up. The contrast between doubt and faith here is stark.

One of our biggest problems in life is to believe in God and what He says. The problem is that we do not often recognize this to be the problem. (This is discussed further in chapter 4). The apostles all struggled to believe, and as we see, Jesus was quick to address their lack of faith because He knew how important their faith was. Thomas of course was the most famous doubter because he refused to believe the other ten apostles and gave an unrealistic condition for him to begin to believe in the resurrection of the Lord. Amazingly, the Lord accommodated his request and graciously appeared to Thomas.

Now Thomas, called the Twin, one of the twelve, was not with them when Jesus came. The other disciples therefore said to him, "We have seen the Lord." So he said to them, "Unless I see in His hands the print of the nails, and put my finger into the print of the nails, and put my hand into His side, **I will not believe**." And after eight days His disciples were again inside, and Thomas with them. Jesus came, the doors being shut, and stood in the midst, and said, "Peace to you!" Then He said to Thomas, "Reach your finger here, and look at My hands; and reach your hand here, and put it into My side. **Do not be unbelieving, but believing.**" And Thomas answered and said to Him, "My Lord and my God!" Jesus said to him, "Thomas, because you have seen Me, you have believed. Blessed are those who have not seen and yet have believed." (John 20:24–29)

For a long time, Jesus had been attempting to train His apostles to walk by faith, but it was quite a task. We see even back in Mark 4:40 that they were fearful and doubted: "But He said to them, 'Why are you so fearful? **How is it that you have no faith?**'"

My opinion is that the apostles did not fully overcome their fear and doubt until they received the Holy Spirit (John 20:22; were born again, John 3:3, 7) and the power of the Spirit (Acts 1:8, 2:4). Subsequent chapters in the book of Acts reveals great testimonies of the apostles moving in great faith. Hallelujah! Thank God for the move of His Spirit in our lives by His grace, amen.

Conclusion

If only God's people would be obedient and learn to walk by faith (2 Cor. 5:7), nothing on this planet would be able to stop His church (Mark 9:23; Matt. 17:20).

> I will build My church, and the gates of Hades shall not prevail against it. (Matt. 16:18)

And God declared His people were unbeatable.

> No weapon formed against you shall prosper, and every tongue which rises against you in judgment you shall condemn. (Isa. 54:17)

> If you believe ... nothing will be impossible for you! (Matt. 17:20)

What a great vision of a victorious church! It is all by grace through faith that no man may boast before the Lord of the universe (Eph. 2:8–9; Zech. 4:6–7).

How Do I Respond?

Let us be careful not to allow unrealistic expectations to allow doubts to grow, to focus excessively on them, or to allow our faith to remain immature (R. C. Sproul).

Remember the character of doubt; do not let doubt condemn you. Doubt can be a useful stepping stone to a greater faith. Anticipate and resist the confusion, uncertainty, and fog that can come from a doubtful feeling. Specifically address the underlying questions and issues that are causing the doubt.

Let's move on from doubt to faith, from weakness to strength, from lack to blessings, from the wilderness into the Promised Land to see many leaders rise up and many churches grow and multiply, to see our countries impacted by the power of God. We serve an awesome, wonderful God who created all life and the entire universe, who died to save us from our transgressions, who deserves everyone to honor Him, amen!

Chapter Summary

How important is your faith in God to you?
My faith in God and in His Word is the most important possession I can have in this world.
The apostle Paul prayed that he might perfect what was lacking in their faith.

Doubt can be the biggest enemy in our lives.

The strength of our faith can be revealed by the doubts and fears we are able to overcome.

References

R. C. Sproul. 1993. "Addressing our Doubts Leads to Certainty."

Eugene Myers Harrison. 1945. "J. Hudson Taylor: God's Mighty Man of Prayer." https://www.wholesomewords.org/missions/biotaylor3.html.

CHAPTER 4
Overcoming Self-Doubt

Night and day praying exceedingly that we may see your
face and perfect what is **lacking in your faith**.

—1 Thessalonians 3:10

In early 2019, two women came forward at our Hope Church in Perth for prayer. One had been in hospital a few days previously with excruciating back pain, and the other had had back pain on and off for over twenty years due to a damaged disk. I prayed for them, and initially, there was no sign of relief of pain. The first claimed the pain was "only" five out of ten (ten being the max) and the other was three out of ten. After some minutes, the second woman began to smile indicating that there was an improvement in her mobility and she was "feeling something." The first still had no change. Tough case. I began to rebuke any spirits of doubt, etc., that might be hindering us from receiving from God. I was following the Francis Hunter model and commanding the nerves to move into the correct location so as not to be pinched as well as alignment of bones, etc.

After maybe ten minutes of prayer, the second woman claimed that she could rotate her neck without pain, something she couldn't do before. That encouraged the first woman, who kept praying and agreeing for her healing. After about another five minutes, a smile burst across her face (priceless to watch) as she said she felt the pain leave. Praise the Lord! God is still doing miracles today by His grace, amen.

God is telling us that we can move mountains!

So Jesus answered and said to them, "Have faith in God. For assuredly, I say to you, whoever says to **this mountain**, 'Be removed and be cast into the sea,' and **does not doubt in his heart**, but **believes** that those things he says will be done, he will have whatever he says. Therefore I say to you, whatever things you ask when you pray, **believe** that you receive them, and you will have them." (Mark 11:22–24)

God is telling us that we can be overcomers, amen!

For whatever is born of God **overcomes** the world. And this is the victory that has **overcome** the world—our faith. Who is he who **overcomes** the world, but he who believes that Jesus is the Son of God? (1 John 5:4–5)

But how many of us complain when faced with mountains and when we don't feel like overcomers? Instead, we act like Gideon, using words such as *if ... why? ... where? ... forsaken ... how? ... weakest ... least ...* Sounds like us, doesn't it? Then he mutters, "Show me a sign." I think we can all relate to these words at some stage or other in our different levels of spiritual development and process of maturity.

And the Angel of the Lord appeared to him, and said to him, "The Lord is with you, you mighty man of valor!" Gideon said to Him, "O my lord, **if** the Lord is with us, **why** then has all this happened to us? And w**here** are all His miracles which our fathers told us about, saying, 'Did not the Lord bring us up from Egypt?' But now the Lord has **forsaken** us and delivered us into the hands of the Midianites." Then the Lord turned to him and said, "Go in this might of yours, and you shall save Israel from the hand of the Midianites. Have I not sent you?" So he said to Him, "O my Lord, **how** can I save Israel? Indeed my clan is the **weakest** in Manasseh, and I am the **least** in my father's house." And the Lord said to him, "Surely I will be with you, and you shall defeat the Midianites as one man." Then he said to Him, "If now I have found favor in Your sight, then **show me a sign** that it is You who talk with me." (Judg. 6:12–17)

When we are doubting, in bondage and difficulty, we ask the same questions, "If the Lord is with us ... where are all His miracles? ... The Lord has forsaken us! ... How can I ... the weakest ... I am the least? ... Show me a sign, God!" These are the words of those struggling to believe that God can deliver them, those who have been assailed by doubt and are hiding in wine presses for fear of the enemy. When have we ever found ourselves hiding from the enemy? I remember once in 1989, I felt so defeated that I didn't even want to get out of bed. It was a bad day.

O'Donovan (2018) stated, "If you are lacking self confidence in an area, there is almost always a limiting belief hidden somewhere that keeps holding you back ... your external world starts to change based on your internal world." Let's begin to address these limiting beliefs and start to speak to some mountains and assert that we are overcomers. We can become aware of our thoughts and beliefs, change our limited thinking, and compare ourselves to others less and less.

Initially, Moses Also Had a Lot of Doubt

We see in Exodus that initially, Moses tried to avoid God's mission for him about five times due to his doubts, insecurity, and uncertainty about his abilities.

> **Who am I** that I should go to Pharaoh, and that I should bring the children of Israel out of Egypt? ... Indeed, when I come to the children of Israel and say to them, "The God of your fathers has sent me to you," and they say to me, "What is His name?" **what shall I say** to them? ... But suppose **they will not believe me** or listen to my voice; suppose they say, "The Lord has not appeared to you." ... O my Lord, **I am not eloquent**, neither before nor since You have spoken to Your servant; but I am slow

of speech and slow of tongue … O my Lord, **please send**
by the hand of whomever else You may send. (Ex. 3:11ff,
4:1, 10, 13)

It is amazing that Moses even obeyed God and left the desert of
Midian to travel back to Egypt. It is surprising that he became such a great
man of faith after such a shaky start. Most of us would have given up, but
Moses pressed into God and began to see His miracles revealed in Egypt,
so he gained courage and listened to and obeyed the Lord. As he did this,
he saw greater and greater miracles. Wonderful! The amazing quality about
the Lord is that He does not show favoritism; if Moses met the conditions
of holiness, obedience, and faith, so can we, and in that case, we too can
see the miraculous in our lives, amen!

While I was a PhD student in the School of Physics at Melbourne
University, I prayed for a technical assistant who complained that he had
hurt his thumb. The next day, I asked him how his thumb was feeling, and
he said it was worse. Don't let the disappointments of the past hold us back.
In early 2020, a woman in our church in Adelaide came forward for prayer
and received healing for terrible back pain and other nervous system issues
that had been so bad that she had not slept properly or walked without pain
for twenty years. She said she was healed before I had finished praying!

The encouraging lesson from Moses's example is that at first, he did
not think he could do what God had asked him to do; he doubted and
prevaricated, but he overcome these initial problems, and so can we. Often,
we don't feel equipped to serve God, but consider what He has already
provided us!

Now we have received, not the spirit of the world, but the
Spirit who is from God, that we might know the things
that have been freely given to us by God. (1 Cor. 2:12)

The apostle Paul told us that the Spirit of God would show us the
things God has already given us. What would some of these things be? We
see in the blessings in Ephesians 1:3 and in 2 Peter 1:3 that He has given
us all the things we need.

> Blessed be the God and Father of our Lord Jesus Christ, who has blessed us with every spiritual blessing in the heavenly places in Christ. (Eph. 1:3)

> His divine power has given to us all things that pertain to life and godliness, through the knowledge of Him who called us by glory and virtue. (2 Pet. 1:3)

The Human Brain vs. Supercomputers … Which One Wins?

But what has God given us? Let's look at the brain God has given us. Which is more powerful—your brain or the world's fastest supercomputer? David Eagleman said that the human brain was faster than "dozens of the world's fastest supercomputers" (Eagleman 2016).

> The human brain is far more advanced and efficient, and possesses more raw computational power than the most impressive supercomputers that have ever been built. (Staughton 2019)

In 2014, researchers in Japan matched the processing power in one second from 1 percent of the brain with the fourth fastest supercomputer in the world (the K computer). It took forty minutes to perform the calculations for a single second of 1 percent of human brain activity! (Wilkinson 2013).

Over 1,000 electrical connections per neuron with about 100 billion neurons make the human brain a phenomenal hive of electrical activity with over 100 trillion electrical connections. No wonder I am fearfully and wonderfully made (Ps. 139:14). How can evolution possibly explain the irreducible complexity resident in our brains? (See *Darwin's Black Box* by Professor Michael Behe.) If God can give us such a powerful brain, we can apprehend the power of the Holy Spirit that He has freely provided for us (John 7:37–38) and achieve great things for Him.

Tips to Overcome Self-Doubt

Have faith in Jesus Christ, the Son of God (1 John 5:13).

Learn to trust in God (Isa. 26:3), not your own ability, and rely on Him to help you (Ps. 50:15).

Learn what God says about us as His children (Rom. 8:31, 37).

Be focused about what you want to do; have a clear vision (Prov. 29:18).

Make sure the Lord's blessing will be upon your work (Rom. 12:2, knowing God's will; 1 John 5:14,15).

Develop a clear action plan (2 Cor. 1:17).

Be diligent and work hard (Prov. 12:27).

Don't listen to negative people (1 Cor. 15:33).

Persevere when the going gets tough (Heb. 10:35–36).

Go for it! Overcome setbacks (1 John 5:4).

Do it for Jesus (Col. 3:23).

Be a success; be the best you can be (Rom. 15:18–20).

Remain humble, and give all the glory to God (Rev. 4:9–11).

Conclusion

Gideon and Moses struggled with doubt and feelings of inadequacy, but God is encouraging us that He has given us all things we need for this life to be overcomers and to share in His divine nature. As briefly described above, the human brain is a miracle that we live with and utilize every day; let us meditate on the power of God and His potential to work in our lives today.

How Do I Respond?

Recognize that self-doubt affects all of us but that we can overcome it.

Begin to apply the Word of God to our thinking.

Begin to take captive every thought that derides us or makes us feel inferior.

Begin to take away traditional limits you have placed on yourself.

Ask God what He would like you to do for Him.

Trust in God to do greater things in your life, amen!

Chapter Summary

God is telling us that we can move mountains.

God is telling us that we can be overcomers, amen!

Can I do what God is calling me to do? Yes!

The human brain is faster than "dozens of the world's fastest supercomputers"!

References

Kirstin O'Donovan. 2018. "Is Your Self Confidence Affecting Your Job Performance?" http://www.lifehack.org/articles/work/is-your-self-confidence-affecting-your-job-performance.html.

David Eagleman. 2016. "The Brain The Story of You."

Jens Wilkinson. 2013. "Largest neuronal network simulation achieved using K computer." http://www.riken.jp/en/pr/press/2013/20130802_1/z.

John Staughton. 2019. "The Human Brain vs. Supercomputers ... Which One Wins?" https://www.scienceabc.com/humans/the-human-brain-vs-supercomputers-which-one-wins.html.

Michael J. Behe. 1996. "Darwin's Black Box: Biochemical Challenge to Evolution."

CHAPTER 5
Your Faith Determines Your Future

Having been **justified by faith**, we have peace
with God through our Lord Jesus Christ.

—Romans 5:1

W hat I believe determines how I respond to every circumstance I find
myself in. Jeremiah was in Jerusalem just before 586 BC, when the
city was destroyed and burned, yet he was able to declare a "future and a
hope" for those who will trust in God!

> After seventy years are completed at Babylon, I will visit
> you and perform **My good word toward you,** and cause
> you to return to this place. For I know the thoughts that
> I think toward you, says the Lord, **thoughts of peace**
> and not of evil, **to give you a future and a hope.** Then
> you will call upon Me and go and pray to Me, and I will
> listen to you. And you will seek Me and find Me, when
> you search for Me with all your heart. I will be found by
> you, says the Lord, and **I will bring you back from your
> captivity.** (Jer. 29:10–14)

Faith in God gives us hope when nothing else around us can or does.
Jeremiah was revealing God's heart and plan for His people to give them
a future and a hope and to bring them back from their captivity. What a

Dr. Brendan Kirby

great word for people about to go into bondage to their captors. Daniel prayed fervently some seventy years later (Dan. 9:2–3) that the Lord would bring this word to pass, which He graciously did (Zech. 1:12, 16; Ezra 1:1–2).

Do we believe God can bring us out of our captivity into a place flowing with "milk and honey," a place flowing with rivers of living water of love, joy, and peace?

Viktor Frankl, an Austrian psychologist, survived the death camps of Nazi Germany during World War II. While incarcerated, Frankl made an amazing discovery about why some survived the horrible conditions and why some did not. Frankl looked at various factors—health, vitality, family structure, intelligence, survival skills, and so on, but he concluded that the single most significant influence was a sense of vision, an impelling conviction the survivors had that they had a mission to perform, some important work left to do. "Survivors of POW camps in Vietnam and elsewhere have reported similar experiences: *a compelling, future-oriented vision* is the primary force that kept many of them alive," Steve Covey (1996) said. The people who survived believed that there was a meaning and significance in life that they were meant to fulfill.

Frankl went on to write *Man's Search for Meaning*, (1946), a best-selling book based on what he learned and experienced. In it, he wrote, "Everything can be taken from a man but one thing: the last of the human freedoms—**to choose one's attitude in any given set of circumstances**, to choose one's own way." This can also be applied to our faith today. No matter whether we are in a holocaust concentration camp or just having a miserable day, we can choose to have faith that the God who created the universe can turn our circumstances around for our good and for His glory, amen!

The people of Israel believed they were in bondage and captivity. The word *Egypt*, known in Hebrew as *mitzraim*, is synonymous with bondage and servitude (Levi 2015). Egypt is also known by the word *maw-tsore*, a place of confinement or a besieged place, with synonyms such as fortified defense, siege, enclosure, limitation—with a literal meaning of bondage or slavery (www.biblestudytools.com).

Therefore they set taskmasters over them to afflict them with their burdens. And they built for Pharaoh supply cities, Pithom and Raamses. But the more they afflicted them, the more they multiplied and grew. And they were in dread of the children of Israel. So the Egyptians made the children of Israel serve with rigor. And **they made their lives bitter with hard bondage**—in mortar, in brick, and in all manner of service in the field. All their service in which they made them serve was with rigor. (Ex. 1:11–14)

Pringle (2006) stated,

Israel experienced about 300 years of bondage and slavery after Joseph's death. No salary. No income. No ownership of land or anything. No hope for a future. Nowhere to go. The only expectation was to be a slave again tomorrow – with perhaps one less whip mark on their back.

But did they believe the promise of God that they would be set free one day?

Hebrews 3:19, 4:2 states that it was because of unbelief that they did not enter; they refused to believe it possible. Psalm 78:41 says that the Israelites repeatedly "tempted God and limited the Holy One of Israel." The tragedy is this—How many of us miss out on what God has for each of us because we limit God as those Israelites did by our unbelief?

A few hundred years later during the time of judges, while Samson judged Israel, the Israelites came to Samson and pleaded with him exclaiming, "Do you not know that the Philistines rule over us?" (Judg. 15:11). Similarly, people today can be slow to believe that escape from sin is possible (Rom. 6:18, 22).

We were all in a place of slavery, a type of Egypt, at one time or another in our lives. Today, our place of slavery is the flesh. Romans and Galatians speak about waging war with the flesh (Gal. 5:17) and having our minds set on the flesh (Rom. 8:5–8). The fruit of the flesh are the consequences of our sinful habits as outlined in Galatians 5:19–21. The beauty of the sacrifice of the Son of God on the cross is that we are now "set free from sin" (Rom. 6:14, 18, 22). Is it not glorious to have the spiritual power and authority imparted to us to be set free from all entangling bondages of our sinful nature? Thank God! But do those still practicing their sin actually believe they will ever be free?

> Jesus answered them, "Most assuredly, I say to you, whoever commits sin is **a slave of sin** … Therefore if the Son makes you free, you shall be free indeed." (John 8:34, 36)

> He has delivered us **from the power of darkness** and conveyed (translated) us into the kingdom of the Son of His love, in whom we have redemption through His blood, the forgiveness of sins. (Col. 1:13–14)

> While they promise them liberty, they themselves are **slaves of corruption**; for by whom a person is overcome, by him also he is brought into bondage. (2 Pet. 2:19)

What I believe about sin and whether it has the ability to capture and control me affects my future. How can God use people who lack faith to overcome their old natures as examples for others? Sin will destroy my future. Faith in God and commensurate obedience to His purposes will ensure my success: "And this shall come to pass if you diligently obey the voice of the Lord your God" (Zech 6:19c).

My faith in Jesus Christ and His death and resurrection (as described in John 8:34, 36, and Col. 1:13 above) takes me out of slavery to bad habits into the liberty of His Spirit (Gal. 5:1). Ultimately, it is my decision and determination to appropriate the liberty bought for me by Jesus Christ as to whether I allow sin to rule in my life or not.

I have been there myself; I know what it is like to be bondage. But as I have experienced, the "needle" needs to be pulled out, not sympathized with. Believe me, I have shed more tears than most people. In 1987, I fell into a romantic bondage with a young girl in our church, and I could not stop thinking about her. I was a young Christian and inexperienced in the spiritual warfare associated with this pattern of thinking. The infatuation and imaginary relationship almost drove me mad, and her subtle rejection of me broke my heart twice in two years. At one stage, I was so weak that I thought I would never escape the clutches of this bondage. It took almost four and a half years of struggle before I began to really overcome and get back to normal strength again.

The classic statement of a defeatist mentality is illustrated by the Israelites approaching Samson, who had dared believe that God had power to deliver Israel from its enemies (Heb. 11:32–33).

> Then three thousand men of Judah went down to the cleft of the rock of Etam, and said to Samson, "**Do you not know that the Philistines rule over us?** What is this you have done to us?" (Judg. 15:11)

This was an amazing lack of faith in God and acquiescence to the status quo. Some may compromise with their situation and exclaim, "Don't you know that I've had this problem for many years? It won't just go away. I've tried!" But faith apprehends the promises of God, amen! The Bible says we are set free from every debilitating weakness (Heb. 12:1). Therefore, let us fight (1 Tim. 6:12; 2 Tim. 4:7) to inherit what we believe is possible according to the Word of God, what He has already promised us (Heb. 6:12).

Abraham grew strong in faith to receive what God had promised. Many of us try to receive what God has not clearly promised. He has not promised a trouble-free life, or necessarily that cute person we fell in love with, or to make us all rich, or to give each of us a Mercedes-Benz. But He has promised to provide for all our needs in Christ Jesus (Phil. 4:19), to answer our cry for help in our time of trouble (Ps. 50:15; Jer. 33:3), and to help us to overcome every bad habit and the sin that so easily besets us (Heb. 12:1). He has promised to empower us to do His will for our lives (Acts 1:8).

We have all been in a place of weakness at one time or another. I was so weak when enduring my romantic trial, but I maintained a hope in God that He would bring me through whether my hopes would be realized or not. I believed God would do a good work in me (Phil. 1:6). I spoke to a famous apostle once that "out of weakness," He will make me strong!

> ... who through faith ... obtained promises ... out of weakness were made strong ... (Heb. 11:33, 34)

Joseph was in slavery and prison for almost thirteen years, but he believed God would deliver him and bring to pass the dream that God had given him even though he did not know when he would be released.

Daniel found himself in a lions' den (Dan. 6:16), but he believed God would protect him.

Job lost everything (Job 2:10) but maintained his faith and trust in God and his integrity (Job 13:15), and out of his pitiful weakness of despair and self-righteous complaining, the Lord delivered him and revealed His glory to him (Job 42:5–6).

Jeremiah stood before the princes of King Jehoiakim as they discussed his death (Jer. 26:11), but he stood his ground believing in God for support and received his own life as a reward whereas the prophet Urijah fled from King Jehoiakim to Egypt and died for his fear (Jer. 26:23).

Our faith in the strength that God provides us to help us in our time of need can take us out from weakness to a place of confidence, hope, and power.

The Promises of God Are Inherited by the Good Fight of Faith

> This charge I commit to you, son Timothy, according to the prophecies previously made concerning you, that **by them you may wage the good warfare.** (1 Tim. 1:18)

> **Fight the good fight of faith**, lay hold on eternal life, to which you were also called and have confessed the good confession in the presence of many witnesses. (1 Tim. 6:12)

> I have **fought the good fight**, I have finished the race, I
> have kept the faith. (2 Tim. 4:7)

Warfare is an important component of walking by faith. We need to fight
our doubts, fears, confusion, and anxieties and not let them rob us of what
God wants to give us by faith. This is not easy, and many shrink from
fighting their own sinful thoughts and tendencies.

Joshua was commanded (perhaps up to six times) to be strong and
of good courage so that he could lead the people of Israel into the land
promised to them by God. Even when he felt like giving up after the
terrible defeat at Ai (Josh. 7:7), God told him to get up, to stop feeling
sorry for himself, and specifically to address the problem (Josh. 7:10–11).
The devil will attempt to confuse and deceive us with our "feelings" (Rev.
20:3; 1 Cor. 14:33), but the Lord convicts and directs us specifically by
His Spirit (John 16:8). To inherit the Promised Land, Joshua and his army
needed to fight and overcome the giants in that land (Heb. 6:12).

Your Faith Determines Your Future

> And when He had come into the house, the blind men
> came to Him. And Jesus said to them, "Do you believe
> that I am able to do this?" They said to Him, "Yes, Lord."
> Then He touched their eyes, saying, **"According to your
> faith let it be to you."** And their eyes were opened. (Matt.
> 9:28–30)

Faith here brings about victory over blindness, hallelujah! But what if I do
not have sufficient faith? Jesus said in Matthew 17:19–20 that the apostles
did not have success because of their little faith. Peter began to sink into
the water because his faith weakened when he looked at his circumstances
(Matt. 14:30–31).

But Jesus said, "According to your faith let it be to you!" (Matt.
9:29) and "As you have believed, so let it be done for you" (Matt. 8:12).
Are we ready for this? Can we accept responsibility for our futures? This
also means that we do not just give a theological loop and say that God

is in control of my future and the will of the Lord will be done. Yes, this is true, but it is dependent on our choices, faith, and decisions. Because God knows the future does not mean that we delegate it to Him. God has commanded us to do certain things He has delegated to us (for example, Matt. 28:19–20), which we cannot counter-delegate back up to Him to do.

One example from scripture where God expected us to work with Him involved the inheritance of the Promised Land by God's people. Numbers 14 shows us that the first generation failed completely. God waited for a second generation to rise up to work with Joshua by faith.

> Moses My servant is dead. Now therefore, arise, go over this Jordan, you and all this people, to the land which I am giving to them—the children of Israel. Every place that the sole of your foot will tread upon I have given you, as I said to Moses. (Josh. 1:2–3)

Joshua was told by God to rise up to a new level of courage and faith! Faith obeys God's Word and believes in God's promises.

> This Book of the Law shall not depart from your mouth, but you shall meditate in it day and night, that you may observe to do according to all that is written in it. For then you will make your way prosperous, and then you will have good success. Have I not commanded you? Be strong and of good courage; do not be afraid, nor be dismayed, for the Lord your God is with you wherever you go. (Josh 1:8–9)

Faith leads us into victory (1 John 5:4; 2 Cor. 2:14). Joshua believed the Word of God and went on to achieve great success for Jesus by conquering the enemies of the Lord. What enemy of God is affecting our lives right now? God is commanding us to overcome it by faith as Joshua did.

Faith believes what God has given us; 1 Corinthians 2:12 reads, "Now we have received, not the spirit of the world, but the Spirit who is from

God, that we might know the things that have been freely given to us by God."

Faith meditates upon and obeys the Word of God. God wants us to prosper and be successful so that we can extend His kingdom, amen. We must believe that God is with us and be strong and courageous.

What level of faith and courage are we at today? What do we believe we can achieve in our lives? Will we let our fears, doubts, anxieties, and stress lead us and cause us to sink below mediocrity, or will we press on by faith (Hab. 2:4) and achieve great things for God in this temporary world?

Hebrews 10:36 tells us, "Now the just shall live by faith; but if anyone draws back, My soul has no pleasure in him."

When confronted with the armies of Edom, Moab, and Ammon, King Jehoshaphat of Judah declared a time of fasting and prayer. After receiving the word of the Lord through Jahaziel, he encouraged his people to believe in God and to believe the prophetic word. Faith here was the key to victory, not a brilliant military strategy (although that can be a good thing). The key words Jehoshaphat used were to *believe* and *be established*. Perhaps a hundred years later, Isaiah used the same principle in reverse wording. It is up to us to believe, obey, and act, and then we will be established.

> Hear me, O Judah and you inhabitants of Jerusalem: Believe in the Lord your God, and **you shall be established**; believe His prophets, and you shall prosper. (2 Chron. 20:20)

> If you will not believe, surely you shall not be established. (Isa. 7:9)

Some people do not inherit God's best for them. If we find a detailed Bible commentary, we can see that the Promised Land extended geographically significantly farther than what the children of Israel actually conquered. Although they did achieve great victories and conquered large swaths of enemy territory, it was not all that God had for them; it was in reality not God's best (see Josh. 13:1, 18:3; Judg. 1:27, 29–34, 2:20–23). Sometimes, we allow the enemy into our land and do not completely drive them out of our souls. Consequently, we do not inherit all that God has for us.

Some of our most dangerous enemies are doubt, fear, anxiety, stress, and worry, but we often accept them as part of our lives not knowing that they erode our faith in God and limit His work in our lives. Some of us are so trained to doubt and fear that it is hard to reconcile a future for our hearts without these influences. How can we learn to hate these enemies of God and drive them out of our souls?

There is hope. God is a God of hope and faith, and faith is the substance of things hoped for (Heb. 11:1). Romans 15:13 reads, "Now may the God of hope fill you with all joy and peace in believing, that you may **abound in hope** by the power of the Holy Spirit."

The Lord can help us through our weaknesses and bring us into a place of faith and strength.

Conclusion

God wants us to first understand how faith operates and then walk in faith and grow stronger in faith so we can receive what He wants to give us by faith. We receive very little from God except by faith.

Doubt and fear do not receive from God. Stubbornness and sinful habits cannot receive from God. Humility and commitment to Jesus is our starting point to grow in faith and get to a place of strong faith, where the promises of God are received, amen!

How Do I Respond?

Determine to grow in faith today. The apostle Paul told us that whatever was not from faith was sin (Rom. 14:23). James told us that if we know what to do and we do not do it, that is a sin (James 4:17). These two scriptures give those of us wanting to do better in our lives a good starting point. We must firstly clean up our hearts under the guidance of the Holy Spirit (Pss. 139:23–24, 19:14; 1 John 3:21). It requires a lot of effort and determination to overcome our selfish natures, but with prayer and fasting, all things are possible. Then with a clear vision (Prov. 28:19) start training ourselves to think positively. As Joel Osteen (2004) reminded us,

Until we learn how to enlarge our vision, seeing the future through our eyes of faith, our own wrong thinking will prevent good things from happening in our life … We must stop dwelling on negative, destructive thoughts that keep us in a rut. Our life is not going to change until we first change our thinking.

Chapter Summary

What I believe determines how I respond to my current situation.

The people of Israel believed they were in bondage and captivity.

My faith in Jesus Christ and His death and resurrection takes me out of slavery to bad habits into the liberty of His Spirit.

God's promises are inherited by the good fight of faith.

Our faith determines our future.

Determine to grow in faith today.

References

Stephen Covey. 1996. *First Things First*, 103. Fireside.

Levi. 2015. Definition of *mitzraim* http://learntorah.blogspot.com/2015/01/egypt-means-bondage-in-hebrew.html.

Maw-tsore. Definition of, https://www.biblestudytools.com/lexicons/hebrew/nas/matsowr-3.html.

Joel Osteen. 2004. *Your Best Life Now.* Faithwords.

Viktor Frankl. 1946. *Man's Search for Meaning.*

Phil Pringle. 2006. Sermon outline, C3 Oxford Falls.

CHAPTER 6
Inheriting the Promises and Overcoming the Seven Enemies of Our Faith

> For the Son of God, Jesus Christ, who was preached among
> you by us—by me, Silvanus, and Timothy—was not Yes and
> No, but in Him was Yes. For **all the promises of God** in Him
> are Yes, and in Him Amen, to the glory of God through us.
>
> —2 Corinthians 1:19–20

Visit to Kaniola, DRC

During a trip to the eastern state of South Kivu of the Democratic Republic of Congo (DRC) in 2008 to visit Ps. Kanigi Mapya and his churches, I wanted to get a feel for more than just the central churches in Bukavu, so we traveled the countryside visiting a number of the churches there. DRC had been working its way out of a terrifying civil war that had claimed the lives of over 5 million. Bukavu had been destroyed in the fighting and was still being rebuilt. The people were still traumatized and shaken; they were slowly putting their lives back in order. Into this tense setting I flew in quite unaware of what I was getting into.

While we were on the way to visit the church in Kaniola, a rural village outside Bukavu, two Congolese army soldiers stopped our old four-wheel drive thinking that I was a rebel. Numerous white men had entered the country as mercenaries and had been shooting people as part of the rebel forces. Congolese soldiers have incredible impunity in DRC;

I am told that they can do whatever they like and the local police cannot touch them. I was sitting in the front seat taking a few photos with my digital camera admiring the trees, grassy hills, and birds in flight. It was a beautiful panorama in the early afternoon. I thought the soldiers were just chatting with Ps. Mapya. But about four years later, Mapya told me that they had wanted to shoot me! Ps. Mapya had told the soldier, "If you shoot the muzungu (the white man), then you have to shoot all of us." Fortunately for me and for all of us, they decided to let us continue on our missionary journey.

Mapya told this story to Ps. Wilson and me in September 2016. He said, "I gave my promise to God to protect you, so that is what I had to do. We must be ready to die!" Such faith is unusual today. How is our faith today? Are we willing to die like Ps. Mapya for our faith in Jesus Christ?

A promise is a psychological contract in which a person undertakes to render some service or gift to another or devotes something valuable for his use. It may also be any vow or guarantee. God makes many promises to us usually that are conditional on various levels of our obedience and faithfulness.

The Lord gave Abraham the promise of a child to inherit the land after him (Gen. 12:1–3), but there was a bigger promise behind God's plan, which led God to test and develop Abraham's faith to a higher level so that He could pass a stricter test (Gen. 22:1) and inherit an eternal promise of his seed, Christ (Gal. 3:16), the Messiah, to save the world. What a promise!

Without weakening in his faith, Abraham faced the fact that his body was as good as dead since he was about a hundred years old and Sarah's womb was also dead. Yet he did not waver through unbelief at the promise of God but was strengthened in his faith and gave glory to God being fully persuaded that God had power to do what He had promised (Rom. 4:20,21).

The prophet Isaiah told us to emulate the "rock from which we were hewn and the hole from which we were dug," that is, Abraham's example of faith (Isa. 51:1–2). The apostle Paul told us that Abraham was the father of all those who believed, the father of all nations, the father of circumcision, and the father of us all (Rom 4:11–12, 16–17), so he is our father of faith. We see from the above scripture that Abraham embodied the qualities of perseverance, not looking at the circumstances, not wavering in unbelief, but focusing on the promise of God and on the trustworthiness of His character. Abraham overcame the enemies of faith and inherited the promises that God gave him, and so can we, amen!

God Is Faithful, and We Can Trust Him

God acts in a consistent manner; His character is predictable. Even Jonah predicted His mercy on the Ninevites when he charged off to Tarshish (Jon. 4:2).

> So he prayed to the Lord, and said, "Ah, Lord, was not this what I said when I was still in my country? Therefore I fled previously to Tarshish; for I know that You are a gracious and merciful God, slow to anger and abundant in lovingkindness, One who relents from doing harm." (Jon. 4:2)

God fulfills His Word (Jer. 1:12) but in His timing and not always according to our expectations.

> Then the Lord said to me, "You have seen well, for I am watching to perform My word." (Jer. 1:12)

This is where waiting in faith and patience is so important (Heb. 6:12; Ps. 27:14).

> … that you do not become sluggish, but imitate those who through faith and patience inherit the promises. (Heb. 6:12)

> Wait on the Lord; be of good courage, and He shall strengthen your heart; wait, I say, on the Lord! (Ps. 27:14)

We know that God does what He promises to do, but we have need of perseverance so after we have done His will, we will receive what was promised (Heb. 10:36).

> For you have need of endurance, so that after you have done the will of God, you may receive the promise. (Heb. 10:36)

Booker T. Washington (1901) gives an example of someone who went to great lengths to fulfill his promise. He described meeting an ex-slave from Virginia in his book *Up from Slavery*.

> I found that this man had made a contract with his master … that the slave was to be permitted to buy himself, by paying so much per year for his body … Notwithstanding that the Emancipation Proclamation freed him from any obligation to his master, this black man walked the greater portion of the distance back to where his old master lived in Virginia, and placed the last dollar, with interest, in his hands. In talking to me about this, the man told me that he knew that he did not have to pay his debt, but that he had given his word to his master, and his word he had never broken. He felt that he could not enjoy his freedom till he had fulfilled his promise.

How Do We Receive What God Has Promised?

Let's receive what He has already given us (1 Cor. 2:12; 2 Cor 1:19, 20).
Let's press on to receive what He is giving us (Phil. 3:14; Heb. 10:36).
Let's seek the Lord for what He wants to give us (Hos. 6:3; Zech. 8:21; Jer. 33:3; Matt. 7:7).

How Do I Receive What God Has Promised? Seven Keys

By faith (Rom. 4:21; John 5:44).
Praying according to His will (Rom. 8:27; 1 John 5:14–15).

Having patience (Eccl. 3:11; Heb. 6:12).
By enduring hardship (James 1:2–4; Heb. 10:36).
With prayer and fasting (Mark 9:29; Matt. 17:20–21).
Walk in peace and abide in Christ (Col. 3:15; John 15:5, 7).
By overcoming the seven enemies of our faith.

We will discuss the seventh of the above keys in more detail, not to diminish the significance of the first six though.

We Must Overcome the Seven Enemies of Our Faith

1. Doubt is one of our worst enemies and is the Achilles heel of many who seek a stronger walk with the Lord but are unaware of how the enemy cuts down their expectations. The apostle James warned us that if we doubted and wavered, we would receive nothing from God (James 1:6–7). If we allow doubt to weaken our faith, we will often struggle to receive from the Lord. We need to be ruthless in taking captive our thoughts (2 Cor. 10:5) that lead us to doubt God's promises. Such doubt has devastating consequences for our lives if we make decisions from a place of doubt.

> But he who doubts is condemned if he eats, because he
> does not eat from faith; for whatever is not from faith is
> sin. (Rom. 14:23)

Here, the apostle Paul warned us that if we practiced our doubts, we were not walking by faith and hence could not receive from God (Heb. 11:6). We practice our doubts when we make decisions and take actions from a place of doubting. The Holy Spirit told Peter to go to Caesarea "doubting nothing" (Acts 10:19, 11:12) to ensure that Peter would lead the first Gentile Pentecost by faith.

2. Unbelief (Heb. 3:18–19) is a blatant rejection of God and His Word and is linked with disobedience. This is a terrible state to fall into and must be avoided at all costs. The people of Israel balked at the command of God to fight those giants in the land of Canaan (Num. 13), became disobedient, and consequently failed to enter the Promised Land (Num. 14). Sometimes, we can miss what God has for us if we reject His Word.

3. Fear (2 Tim. 1:7) can cripple us in so many ways. Our fears must be exposed, addressed, and doggedly overcome to rid them from our lives! Fear caused the great apostle Peter to doubt and to begin to sink into the water (Matt. 14:30–31) even though he had such courage to begin with. Fear is the opposite of faith; we must face our fears little by little to get victory over them and remove them from our hearts.

4. Anxiety in the heart of man causes depression (Prov. 12:25) whereas faith produces confidence, certainty, and peace. The apostle Paul went as far as to encourage us to be anxious for nothing but to pray and practice casting our cares on the Lord (Phil. 4:6–7). Even the Lord exhorted us not to let anxiety attack us (Luke 12:29; Matt. 6:25).

We can overcome this insidious enemy of our spiritual walk that afflicts and limits our faith by casting our cares on Him through consistent prayer each day and by trusting in God and His sovereignty over our lives (Prov. 3:5–6). We know that we are growing in this ability when our level of peace increases (Isa. 26:3). We might go as far as to say that if we are anxious, we are still learning to trust in the Lord. The peace that "surpasses all understanding" (Phil. 4:7) comes after we pray with thanksgiving and practice trusting in God's Word in a greater way.

5. Confusion is clearly not from God, the author of peace (1 Cor. 14:33). Confusion is an uncertainty that cripples us with inaction and leaves us in a fog (Sproul) as to what the purposes of God are. Confusion attacks us when there are numerous options with multiple seemingly persuasive arguments that we cannot at first get our heads around. To make progress, we must identify and address all our questions and doubts and answer them with the facts so that confusion will lift and confidence can grow in our hearts.

Usually, confusion stays if we reject the truth, and then deception begins to grow (2 Thess. 2:10). An emotional response (in rejecting the truth) such as what Governor Festus uttered in Acts 26:24, "Now as he thus made his defense, Festus said with a loud voice, 'Paul, you are beside yourself! Much learning is driving you mad!'" is not satisfactory if we really want to overcome confusion. In our quest for greater faith, we also must pursue the truth since our faith is placed in what is true, and God promises to reveal the truth to us if we will continually seek it.

Governor Felix was not interested in the truth but in getting the apostle Paul to give him some money (Acts 24:25–26). King Agrippa parried the apostle Paul's attempts to convert him due to his own love of pomp and position (Acts 25:23) without honestly assessing his own heart motives; in Acts 26:28, we read, "Then Agrippa said to Paul, 'You almost persuade me to become a Christian.'" Friends, "almost" is really not satisfactory. Hence, we must pursue the truth "wherever it may lead" as written by Professor Antony Flew who after advocating atheism as a famous worldwide speaker for about fifty years forsook atheism at age eighty after revisiting the evidence for a Creator; he wrote *There is A God* (2008).

Flew effectively stated that the weight of scientific evidence was so great that to continue being an atheist would be untenable in the light of the truth he was discovering. This testimony gives credibility to those sharing their faith with others – that even a world famous atheist can change their mind and believe in a Creator!

6. Sin is such a generic problem that we forget that it will affect our inheritance of God's promises. Sin has caused numerous great saints to miss out on a higher calling, from Moses (Num. 20:12) to King David (2 Sam. 12:8) to Josiah (2 Chron. 35:22–25). Committing a sin is the opposite of being obedient. All sin is lawlessness and rebellion against the Lord. King Saul was not fully obedient and became rebellious, and the Lord rejected him (1 Sam. 15:22–23). So if we practice any sin, we are practicing not listening to the Holy Spirit but to a carnal attitude. Faith in its essence is listening to God and obeying Him (Rom. 10:17); hence, any sin corrodes our faith and limits our future in God (Ps. 78:41). We need to always check ourselves because whatever is not from faith is sin (Rom. 14:23).

Sin withholds good things from us (Jer. 5:25), can bring sickness upon our lives (John 5:14), and pushes God away so that He doesn't hear our prayers (Ps. 66:18). Claiming the promise of forgiveness of sin from 1 John 1:8–9 is good, but it is not a license to allow sin to reside in our hearts (Rom 6:2; Heb 6:4-6; 10:26). We all stumble in many ways, but to grow in faith, we must train ourselves to overcome sin and to stumble less often! Otherwise, we stagnate or get worse (John 5:14).

7. Selfish ambition and selfish motives will also weaken our faith since when we pray for things we do not receive, that can degrade our confidence in our prayers (James 4:2–4). We must be careful to discern our motives (1 Cor. 4:5) as selfish ambition with envy can bring many forms of evil (James 3:16).

Of course, the love of money is a root of many forms of evil desires as well (1 Tim. 6:10). Let us be diligent to watch out for man's approval as well since the desire for honor from men and the lure of fame will also diminish our ability to believe in God's Word; in John 5:44, Jesus remonstrated that people could not believe when they desired honor from men.

Selfish motives take our heart's focus away from God, away from "fixing our eyes on Jesus the author and perfector of our faith" (Heb. 12:2 NASB; Col. 3:2) and places it on things of this world, which again leads to weak faith.

Sometimes, our selfish motives are revealed by the fact that we give up on God's ways and pursue our own as did the Jews in Jerusalem while Jeremiah was still wrestling with them to turn back to the Lord while there was still some chance of saving the city: "This is hopeless! Therefore we will walk according to the plans (desires) of our own heart!" (Jer. 8:12).

Making Progress

We will know we are walking by faith when we get better at obeying God's commands and doing whatever is pleasing in His sight, but that is not simple. Our sinful nature fights against the humility and obedience required for this level of spiritual walk (Phil. 2:5). If our hearts do not condemn us and we have peace with God (1 John 3:21–22), we will know we are progressing. So as mentioned before, we must continually test ourselves if we are walking by faith (2 Cor. 13:5) by addressing the above criteria (the seven enemies of our faith) against our hearts with honesty and integrity.

Fight the Good Fight

Dear brothers and sisters, our faith is our most valuable asset. It is more precious than all of our money and worldly possessions (1 Pet. 1:7). Let us appreciate it and nurture it at all costs and be determined to keep these enemies away from our hearts lest our Christian walk become mundane and uneventful.

The apostle Paul fought the good fight (2 Tim. 4:7), and he wanted us to also fight the good fight (1 Tim. 6:12; Obad 1:17) to apprehend and grab hold of eternal life and the promises of God and not be defrauded on the best that the Lord has for each of us, amen!

Conclusion

Let's press in to receive and walk in all that God has given to us. Let's endure and persevere so that after we have done the will of God, we will receive His promises. Let's continue to believe that God's good promises will come to pass in our lives without giving up, amen!

> Even so we speak, not as pleasing men, but God who tests
> our hearts. (1 Thess. 2:4)

How Do I Respond?

What promises of God have you not yet received? Can you identify why not and if there is a delay in God's purposes for your life?

Do you and your family or leadership team have dreams and hopes that you need to seek the Lord about to consecrate them to His will and purpose for your lives so you can inherit the future He has for you?

Can you identify the particular enemies of your faith that are currently attacking you? Are you able to discern these attacks?

Chapter Summary

We can receive what God has promised by receiving what He has given us and what He is currently giving us and by seeking Him for what He wants to give us.

We receive what God has promised by faith, by praying according to His will, by having patience, by enduring hardship, by prayer and fasting, by walking in love and peace, by abiding in Christ, and by overcoming the seven enemies of our faith: doubt, unbelief, fear, anxiety, confusion, sin, and selfish motives (selfish ambitions).

References

Booker T. Washington. 1901. *Up from Slavery.*

Antony Flew. 2008. *There Is a God—How the World's Most Notorious Atheist Changed His Mind.*

CHAPTER 7
Faith to Overcome Failures

Now thanks be to God who always leads us **in triumph** in Christ, and
through us diffuses the fragrance of His knowledge in every place.

—2 Corinthians 2:14 NKJV

You can do great things. Your potential may be unrealized at the
moment, but a latent seed can still grow and produce much fruit!

In August 1989 I started work as a Research Scientist for the CSIRO
Division of Wool Technology in Geelong. After 12 months instead of
making my position permanent (as previously promised two times by
my boss) I was placed on extended probation in order to assess my work
further. After another three months my superiors unofficially sacked me.
(The official letter had not yet been signed off). It was a devastating blow.
After ten years at university it was now all to no avail. I wondered if my life
would ever recover. My reputation would be shattered. I had three months
employment remaining – my research leader did not care if I came to work
or stayed at home for that duration.

After praying to God for my work that night with David Bernard and
friends at a local bible study in Williamstown I received fresh courage. I
arrived the next morning to work at 8am much to the chagrin of my boss,
determined to overturn this decision. For the next three months I worked
as if my life depended upon it – and I prayed like I had never prayed before,
drawing upon all the trust and faith in God that I could. During this time
the assistant chief of division invited me into his office and recommended

that I resign because it would smooth things out – they would not have to sack me and I would not have that "blot" on my record – but I would have to admit that I could not cope with textile research. I felt like I was in the middle of the plot of a Hollywood drama – except my life really was at stake! I rejected the "kind" offer of the assistant chief and he reconciled himself with having at least tried to help me. I was even more determined to show that I could succeed in this work – not knowing what lay ahead. But I prayed and worked – knowing in my heart that somehow God would work things out.

Towards the end of those three months my determination to "save my future" eventually paid off into my being given a three year research fellowship. This was one of the biggest miracles of my life. Subsequent to this God-given deliverance my three line managers still conspired against me by assigning public staff presentations to me they were confident I would do badly in. Those next three years were some of the most intense in my life!

But I held on to the belief that God would give myself and Nick Sokolov (the eccentric but brilliant engineer from *Footscray*) excellent results in our worsted rectilinear combing research project (Dan. 2:21,22). After another two years or so we were actually leading the world in combing production rate research. This remarkable turnaround of events stunned our division, and our research presentations solicited huge interest. Some of the mathematics that was derived during this work was later published in one of the world's leading textile research journals (J.T.I. 95 (2004) 261). This publication established the results on credible international grounds.

God came through and changed my future because I chose to believe and fought for my job, my self-esteem and my faith. It was very difficult, it was extremely stressful, but with God all things were possible.

No matter how defeated you may feel today, despite the rejection and negative words you may have experienced, you can still arise out of your ashes and achieve victory in your life with God's help.

Don't give up. Fight for your future. Fight for your faith. Keep wrestling against your common enemies of fear, anxiety, confusion, doubt, unbelief, sin and self-centredness!

We Can Overcome

Practice having faith for overcoming even in the midst of seeming failure. It might look like everything is collapsing, but faith and trust in God will always triumph over our circumstances. The only failure we encounter is when we give up on God—He will never give up on us. So let's persevere through every trial and test and even apparent failures, and the Lord will help us, amen!

> For a righteous man may fall seven times, and rise again, but the wicked shall fall by calamity. (Prov. 24:16)

So even though we may fail or fall numerous times, let us brush off the dust of the enemy's accusations of failure and rise again in the Lord's grace. The apostle Paul wrote about the importance of forgetting past failures and even past successes and the priority of pressing ahead for the higher calling.

> Not that I have already attained, or am already perfected; but I press on, that I may lay hold of that for which Christ Jesus has also laid hold of me. Brethren, I do not count myself to have apprehended; but one thing I do, forgetting those things which are behind and reaching forward to those things which are ahead, I press toward the goal for the prize of the upward call of God in Christ Jesus. (Phil. 3:12–14)

Some famous people had to endure rejection and misunderstanding before they were successful. Stan Smith was rejected as too awkward and clumsy to be a ball boy in a Davis Cup tennis match, but he went on to become the number one tennis player in the world in 1972. John Creasey received 743 rejections of his novels, but now, he has sold over seventy million of his crime novels. "What will they send me next?" asked Edmund Hillary's gym instructor about the puny school boy now known as the man who conquered Mount Everest. Beethoven's music teacher declared him hopeless at composing, and Albert Einstein's parents feared he was subnormal (White 2013; Robert 2011).

My grade-five teacher told my parents that she thought I would struggle and not make it at high school. After my year-nine midyear report, my sister said, "Well, dad will not get a scientist in his family after all." My year-ten math teacher shook his head and said I would not make it. My father said I had my head in the clouds and wouldn't amount to anything. I've even had church leaders laugh at me. I failed first-term physics in my first year. I failed my fifth-year report. I even failed my probationary year at CSIRO! Also I was heartbroken and devastated in 1987.

Yet I overcame these numerous negative opinions and obstacles and went on to obtain first-class honors in advanced physics in my third and fourth years at the University of Melbourne (1982 and 1983), won a commonwealth postgraduate research scholarship for four years, graduated years before four of my senior postgraduate colleagues with a PhD in applied nuclear physics (working on the world's best proton microprobe at the time) with no corrections (1989), and went on to work as a research scientist in three Australian government research organizations for another twenty-three years. For eight years, I reviewed X-ray research papers for the journal *Physics in Medicine and Biology*. God will help us if we believe and trust in Him.

We can overcome our temporary failures by spending time with the Lord. We can listen to what God says about us. God is our source of strength, and we need to spend time with Him to be renewed and reinvigorated in our vision (Isa. 41:10). Time with God is like sitting under a gentle shower of love and reassurance that washes away disappointing results and hurtful words.

> For whatever is born of God overcomes the world. And
> this is the victory that has overcome the world—our faith.
> Who is he who overcomes the world, but he who believes
> that Jesus is the Son of God? (1 John 5:4–5)

What does being an overcomer mean to you?

At a crusade meeting in Mushweshwe, South Kivu, Eastern DRC, in 1999, Ps. Mapya was preaching to a crowd of about five hundred. Soon, they were praying for the sick, and a mother brought her dead fifteen-year-old daughter. Many were crying and shouting, "Dead!" The Holy Spirit showed Mapya to "hold her hand and lift her up and use My name." He said, "In the name of Jesus, rise up," and grabbed her hand. She suddenly said, "Hallelujah asante Jesu!" "Hallelujah! Thank you, Jesus." Mapya's faith overcame death!

Mapya said, "There are some who do not hear from the Holy Spirit. If you don't hear from the Holy Spirit, then it will be a shame!" The girl who was raised from the dead gave Mapya a present when she was about to get married in 2018. Mapya told me, "Glory to God. When we hear the word of the Holy Spirit, we know we can raise the dead!" We need to train ourselves to listen to the Spirit more and more.

See Ourselves Overcoming and Decide to Work Hard

We must take responsibility for our decisions and errors. We can learn from our mistakes and figure out why we made them instead of being dragged backward by them. We can begin to believe again that we can do the tasks set before us. I actually failed first-term physics in my first year at university. This was such a shock to my system as I was used to being in the upper echelon at school. I needed to take ownership of my indolence and lack of motivation and decide what I wanted to do. I began to see myself doing well again, but I had to work hard.

Redeem Our Minds

Overcoming failure is very difficult. While loud voices around us speak despair and acquiescence to the apparent reality of defeat, the gentle Spirit of God will whisper to our hearts that we can do it. Asking God for new strategies and approaches, for hope where there is none, for clear vision above the darkness, and for sound, logical, and imaginative thinking is a great way to begin to renew our minds against our recent mistakes, failures, and setbacks. How we think determines our way forward; remember that our faith determines our future.

The apostle Paul encouraged us twice (in Ephesians and Romans) to take captive every thought by the power of the Spirit (2 Cor. 10:4–5) and to change our attitude from failure to success.

> **Put off**, concerning your former conduct, **the old man** which grows corrupt according to the deceitful lusts, and **be renewed in the spirit of your mind**, and that you **put on the new man** which was created according to God, in true righteousness and holiness. (Eph. 4:22–24)

We can change our attitudes (renew our minds) and put on the new man, which has victory over all negative thinking, despair, rejection, depression, sin, defeat, inferiority, insignificance, and complacency.

> And do not be conformed to this world, but be transformed by the renewing of your mind, that you may prove what is that good and acceptable and perfect will of God. (Rom. 12:2)

Renewing our minds means changing the way we normally think. What we believe determines what we think. If we can change what we believe, we can work on altering our attitudes.

William James, a nineteenth-century psychologist, stated, "The greatest discovery of my generation is that a human being can alter his life by altering his attitude." What a great quote from someone regarded as the father of American psychology to encourage us that there is still hope for each of us today. God will give us the power to change what we believe, which will enable us to change our attitude; the rest is up to us.

Trust in God, Not Your Gut

Steve Jobs said, "You have to trust in something, your gut, destiny, life, whatever." Jensen (2012) wrote, "Human beings are often irrational, but you should always trust your intuition and your instincts." No. Making choices based on our gut or heart feelings at the time may seem correct and sometimes turn out to be fruitful, but I advise against making this a habit. Our decision making needs to be based on a coherent set of values taken from Jesus's teachings. We need to live by God's Word (2 Cor. 5:7), not by our feelings. Our feelings can lead us astray especially if we react or make important decisions when we are feeling selfish, bitter, angry, or depressed.

Keep Positive Friends

Proverbs 13:20 reads, "He who walks with wise men will be wise, but the companion of fools will be destroyed." Choose to relate closely with wise men and women. Seek out people who have made significant progress along the path to achieving their dreams, and then learn from them. Keep attuned to the wisdom and positive attitude that they emanate. Remember that too much time with foolish people will have a denigrating effect on your life.

We need to be courageous and choose our friends wisely. Some leaders go as far to say, "Show me your friends and I will show you your future." Be friendly with everybody, but don't be close friends with just anybody. Do not confide in or trust in people whom you haven't proven or tested to be people of integrity (1 Tim. 3:10; 2 Tim. 2:2; Phil. 2:22; 2 Cor. 8:22).

In 1 Corinthians 15:33, we read, "Do not be deceived: evil company corrupts good habits." Negative people can drag others down in subtle or even overt ways. Supposedly well-meaning friends can speak destruction to our dreams and hopes. We should all be careful about whom we spend time with.

We Can Do It

In one of the most amazing accounts of perseverance and overcoming difficult circumstances I know of, Chuck Swindoll (2004) wrote about Worral, a man who was bedridden, totally paralyzed, virtually dumb, totally blind, and could move only one finger. Worral accepted his lot and used the ability he had to move his finger to turn a recorder on and off. He eventually went on to write numerous books and magazine articles.

What Has Sport Got to do With Faith?

Sport in some sense looks like a fairly innocuous pastime for those who are idle and can cover the related expenses. But in many ways, it is a beneficial arena where character and determination can be forged and developed. Leadership skills are tested, patience is matured, the ability to keep calm under pressure is developed, clear thinking is highlighted, and the fear of failure is overcome—all important assets in the arsenal of Christians.

If we are alert to the Lord's dealings, we will find that a variety of issues and character flaws can be exposed and addressed through different sporting activities: pride of achievement, the despair of failure, rejection by teammates, performance orientation, acceptance according to talent, and receiving and giving partiality to those who meet the standard are all rife in the sporting world. Not to mention the normal spiritual carnal weaknesses of lust and self-promotion. Therefore, the ostensibly innocuous activity of playing sports can actually be an intense spiritual battleground. There are manifold lessons we can learn from the Lord during sporting activities if we are attentive to the thoughts of our hearts.

When I began playing competitive amateur tennis in 1977, I was in the bottom section of our district, and I was crippled by the fear of double-faulting. Under pressure when all the others on my team were relying on me and with a crowd watching, I would double-fault and could not clinch the win. It was demoralizing. It took me many years of practice and much determination to overcome my fear of double-faulting. Eventually though, I began to make progress, but it was an arduous climb to a more confident level.

In 1988 in Melbourne, our tennis team was playing VTA Pennant Grade 5. We were among the eight teams to make it to the quarter finals out of sixty-four teams. I was up against an accomplished player who thrashed me 6–1 in the first set. I found myself desperate for a positive course of action for the second set. I had been attempting to rally from the baseline against my opponent, but his ground shots were far superior to mine. I began praying frantically. I knew I had to win this match if we were to have a chance of getting through and winning the final. I kept praying, *God, help me please? What do I do now? This guy's killing me!*

One word came to my heart: *Attack!* I couldn't believe it. I responded immediately in my heart, *That's ridiculous! This guy has phenomenal ground shots! He'll rip me apart, and I'll lose by an even greater margin!* Funny how we often think we know better than the Lord.

But in obedience, in the first game of the second set, I served a weak second serve (after faulting the first serve) and then just charged to the net.

I don't have anything to lose, I reasoned. *This guy's destroyed everything else I've attempted.* Surprisingly, my opponent was overcome with shock that this feeble player was rushing the net behind such a weak serve. Distracted, he missed. A minor breakthrough! I did it again on the next point, and again he was unable to play the winner that I dreaded. *This is amazing!* I thought. *God must be helping me!*

I was walking up and back across the baseline and praying between points. After winning my service game, I also began rushing the net after returning serves, and again, he was shocked and unable to adjust to my change in game plan. The tide was turning; momentum and confidence turned my way, and I was able to complete the match with a win! Even this guy's teammates were shocked and surprised that I had won, and they showed me a significant increase in respect after the match. We eventually won that day and went on to win the final—the best team for the year out of sixty-four teams at that level! This is an example of God coming to help with grace and mercy in my time of need. "Ask and you shall receive" (Matt. 7:7). I asked God for help and relied on Him, and He was true to His promise.

Sports, work, and indeed many arenas of life can easily become spiritual training grounds for us where we learn to rely on the Lord, overcome the odds, and achieve success. Hallelujah! The Lord will lead us to triumph if only we learn to rely on Him more and more.

Here is a personal evaluation question: "Do I view failure as an opportunity for growth in the kingdom or as a personal indictment?"

Conclusion

Don't give up! Keep relying on and trusting in the Lord to help you. See yourself as victorious. See yourself winning, doing your best, succeeding. Persevere! You can certainly achieve what God has given you to do, amen!

Nothing can stop us from doing what the Lord has asked us to do (Rom. 8:31). No weapon can stand against us (Isa. 54:17) as we are more than conquerors (Rom. 8:37).

How Do I Respond?

Do I refuse to take a risk because I am afraid to fail?

How will you approach apparent failure in the future? What will be different in your approach to handle the situation?

Chapter Summary

Do I view failure as an opportunity for growth in the kingdom or as a personal indictment?

We can overcome!

Spend time with the Lord.

See yourself overcoming, and decide to work hard.

Redeem your mind.

Trust in God, not your gut.

Keep positive friends

You can do it!

Some failures in our life are essential on our road to eventual success, greater wisdom and victory.

References

Jack White. 2013. "Rejection," https://fineartviews.com/blog/54816/rejection.

Sunil Robert. 2011. "*Never underestimate, anyone, ever*!" http://sunilrobert. com/never-underestimate-anyone-ever/.

William James quote: https://www.verywellmind.com/william-james-biography-1842-1910-2795545.

Keld Jensen. 2012. *Rock Bottom: How Great Leaders Triumph Over Failure.* https://www.forbes.com/sites/keldjensen/2012/08/08/rock-bottom-how-great-leaders-triumph-over-failure/ and also https://www.facebook.com/viralindians.in/videos/1929500977378794/.

Charles R. Swindoll. 2004. *Early In My Ministry, I Met A Man Named Worral.* https://www.sermoncentral.com/illustrations/ sermon-illustration-charles-r-swindoll-stories-faith-18282.

CHAPTER 8
How to Overcome Negative Feelings

Because of unbelief they were broken off, and you **stand by faith**.

—Romans 11:20

On September 18, 1987, I was thrown again into a trial of faith, but that time, it was romantic in nature and took me completely by surprise. Confusion, disorientation, and uncertainty were enemies that I had not encountered on such an intense level. I was swamped by my fears, overcome with despair, devastated, and brokenhearted. It was a nightmare come true. The pain was real and unendurable. My faith and trust, which I had so much confidence in, were in tatters. There were many lessons still to learn.

This is why this journey of faith means so much to me. I slowly regained my strength by constantly meditating and pressing into the Word of God over an intense three years. Without such extended times, I am confident that the sorrow would have overwhelmed me and I would have stepped back into the world amid my confusion. So I set my sights on learning more about God and more about faith and being led by the Spirit. It was a very difficult trial, but I eventually (after about five years) became much stronger because of it.

Consecration to the Lord

The head of the great Kraft Food Corporation struggled to succeed and was discouraged until he dedicated his life to serving the Lord.

> The days passed and the months passed and he fell into despair. He wasn't succeeding. He wasn't making any money. He was just working long and hard with no success. One day, driving those streets, in a cloud of despair, he began talking to his pony. He said, "Paddy, there's something wrong. We're not doing it right. Our priorities are not where they ought to be. Paddy, He says, "Maybe we ought first to serve God and place God first in our lives." When he got home that night, Kraft made a covenant that all the rest of his life he would serve God first. And then he would work as God would direct and open doors and bless" (Van Boeschoten 2008).

Such consecration is foundational when dealing with difficult emotional swings.

> Why are you cast down, O my soul? And why are you disquieted within me? Hope in God; For I shall yet praise Him, The help of my countenance and my God. (Ps. 43:5)

We see here how King David wrestled with his negative feelings that left him cast down. We all have days when our feelings seem to dominate us and we can't seem to shake these headache-inducing moods. There might be a conflict at work, a disappointing result on a project we have labored on, tension in a close relationship, family arguments, or a car crash.

How many of us have had bad days? Usually, if we look back on them, we can determine that our bad days consisted of our feeling bad or having negative feelings about events or words that were spoken. Perhaps a few things went wrong: I dropped and broke my favorite cup, and someone I loved ignored me. Life is full of situations that do not go our way. We choose to feel upset, angry, rejected, bitter, devalued, or unappreciated.

These feelings can lead to a degenerative cycle into more-dangerous feelings such as depression, isolation, despair, loneliness, or failure.

None of us enjoys feeling bad. These bad feelings can be so debilitating that they can lead to poor decision making. Even the prophet Jonah was led to despair, frustration, and intense anger that culminated in his petitioning the Lord three times to end his torment (Jon. 4:3, 8–9).

But these things do not cause us to have bad days; what does is our reaction to them. It is how we think and then how we feel that causes us to have bad days.

A Common Sequence

An incident (perhaps a minor thing) can lead to a negative response, which can lead to negative thinking, which gives rise to negative feelings.

Our first negative response is where the work can begin. Usually, it is just a habitual way of thinking.

We are often tempted to have a negative, defeatist, or critical attitude, and Paul warned us that such temptations were common.

> No temptation has overtaken you except such as is common to man; but God is faithful, who will not allow you to be tempted beyond what you are able, but with the temptation will also make the way of escape, that you may be able to bear it. (1 Cor. 10:13)

Here are some examples. We've been working very hard. Someone makes a critical or insensitive comment about us. Because we are tired, we are susceptible to a lack of compliments and negative thoughts: *I feel that nobody appreciates me for what I do!* This leads to the negative feeling of not being valued.

We're trying hard to make friends. But a person responds harshly or impatiently with us. Perhaps we have had a few people recently treat us roughly, so we are more sensitive than normal. We begin thinking, *I feel that no one likes me!* This then leads to feelings of insecurity and rejection.

We have been applying ourselves to a new venture or a new field of study and want to make a fresh break in life to get ahead. Unfortunately, we keep getting bad results and things aren't adding up. Because we have had a number of setbacks in succession, we are vulnerable to think *I just don't think I'm going to succeed!* This then leads to a terrible feeling—the fear of failure.

We want to be popular and approved by others based on our abilities and talents. We have sought friendship and relationships, but they just don't seem to be working out. This leaves us open to thoughts such as *I feel as though I'm just not good enough for people!* Consequently, we feel inadequate and unworthy.

We have desires and ambitions; we want this person as our marriage partner or want a certain business or career success, but we neglect to determine if it is God's will for us. Then things do not work out. We complain to God and tell Him that He does not love us because He did not give us what we wanted. We become susceptible to think *God You don't care about me and I don't know where You are!* This leads us to the distinct feeling that God is distant from us.

The above examples of sequences of effort, making plans, applying ourselves diligently, and the ensuing disappointing results are common. We have all been there. But how dominating in our lives should these resultant negative feelings be?

Our Feelings Follow Our Thinking

What we meditate upon (Phil. 4:8) will determine how we feel. Our actions may then often follow our feelings. How many phone calls and texts have we sent while we were upset or feeling frustrated? Our actions produce habits that form our character.

Let us take a closer look at the feelings listed above. What is the main theme in each? Ourselves. But how can we control these feelings? They are so powerful. Is it possible to overcome them?

Moses was feeling weary of the burden of caring for people and feeling like giving up.

> So Moses said to the LORD, "Why have You afflicted Your servant? And why have I not found favor in Your sight, that You have laid the burden of all these people

on me? ... I am not able to bear all these people alone, because the burden is too heavy for me. If You treat me like this, please kill me here and now—if I have found favor in Your sight—and do not let me see my wretchedness!" (Num. 11:11, 14–15)

Joshua was feeling despair because of a short-term failure and was questioning whether they were doing the right thing.

And Joshua said, "Alas, Lord GOD, why have You brought this people over the Jordan at all—to deliver us into the hand of the Amorites, to destroy us? Oh, that we had been content, and dwelt on the other side of the Jordan! O Lord, what shall I say when Israel turns its back before its enemies?" (Josh. 7:7–8)

Both Moses and Joshua had their bad feelings. They felt that life had dealt them a blow, that pressures had built up on them, and that they could not cope. They began to question what they were doing. Elijah also felt that "I alone am left" after demonstrating unusual zeal and power for the Lord (1 Kings 19:10, 14). But in each case, we see the Lord being merciful and giving them gentle correction.

Numbers 11:23 reads, "Has the LORD'S arm been shortened? Now you shall see whether what I say will happen to you or not." God was reminding us that His purposes for our lives would come to pass as long as we stayed on track with Him. Psalm 138:8 reads, "The Lord will accomplish that which concerns me" (also see Phil. 1:6).

King David's Feelings for Absalom

After coming back from exile, Absalom began to steal the hearts of the men of Israel (2 Sam. 15:6)—a lesson about loyalty for every church leader. He soon incited a rebellion against his father and attempted a murderous coup to usurp his father. But the Lord thwarted the wise advice of the trusted counselor Ahithophel, and Absalom mistakenly followed the advice of Hushai the Archite. After King David heard the news that Joab, his chief of army, had killed Absalom in battle across the Jordan River, he cried out aloud with intense emotion and grief for his son.

But the king covered his face, and the king cried out with a loud voice, "O my son Absalom! O Absalom, my son, my son!" … Then Joab said … "you love your enemies and hate your friends. For you have declared today that you regard neither princes nor servants; for today I perceive that if Absalom had lived and all of us had died today, then it would have pleased you well." (2 Sam. 19:4–6)

David struggled between his loyalty to Joab and his men and his excessive love for his son, Absalom. When the course of action before David was clear, he prevaricated (evaded the issue) and was obfuscated by his affections. This is a classic example of allowing our feelings to dominate our more discerning course of action. These feelings were on the verge of ruining David's kingdom to the point that Joab threatened that this show of disloyalty toward his own men would lead to more evil than Absalom's whole rebellion had.

We must train ourselves to watch our thought processes and the emotions they stir up. The Lord gives us great examples of men of God in the Bible through the lives of Moses, Johsua, Elijah, and King David—all of whom were highly regarded by the Lord—but their weakness (possibly due to the limitations of the old covenant; 2 Cor. 3:7, 9; Heb. 7:18–19) is also revealed to us as a means for us to apply the greater spiritual power and authority we have under the new covenant (Heb. 7:22; 2 Cor. 3:8–11, 14) to not allow ourselves to be swayed by our feelings but to take every thought captive as the apostle Paul modeled for us (2 Cor. 10:5) and to renew our minds (Eph. 4:23; Rom. 12:2).

Do Not Be Led by Your Feelings

God's Word brings life and blessings, amen! (John 6:63; Isa. 55:10, 11). John Mellor reminded us, "It is not about what I feel. It is all about what I believe!" Similarly, Smith Wigglesworth disciplined himself to live by the Word of God: "I don't go by what I feel. I go by what the word says." If we say to ourselves *I feel like doing this* or *I don't feel like doing that*, we are walking by sight rather than by faith (2 Cor 5:7, 4:18).

When we ask ourselves, *What do I feel like?* our decision making can be subtly swayed and we may not realize how many decisions we make based on our feelings. Proverbs gives us a couple of warnings in this area.

> A fool vents all his feelings, but a wise man holds them back. (Prov. 29:11)

> Do you see a man hasty in his words? There is more hope for a fool than for him. (Prov. 29:20)

> Example: "I feel like being angry." But again, Proverbs 24:29 tells us not to say, "I will do to him just as he has done to me!" and Ecclesiastes 7:9 reads, "Do not hasten in your spirit to be angry, for anger rests in the bosom of fools."

Lonely people tell themselves, *I don't feel like being friendly today* because they are not used to making an effort to be friendly. But Proverbs tell us we must be friendly if we want to build strong friendships and fulfill our needs for acceptance and belonging. Proverbs 18:24 tells us, "A man who has friends must himself be friendly."

One time, someone seated next to me on a plane was eating frenetically as if he hadn't eaten for a week. It looked shocking to me. I felt that this person was repulsive. I looked at myself while I was eating and thought, *Why can't he eat like me?* But then I realized that I was judging him superficially. Perhaps his habit was cultural? I saw my arrogant way of thinking. We must be careful not to show partiality to those who do things like us. I began to watch my feelings in this instance and then the thoughts that led to those feelings; Proverbs 24:23 reads, "It is not good to show partiality in judgment."

We might wish we were rich, but if we pursue riches, are we not putting them above the Lord? In 1 Timothy 6:9, we read, "But those who desire to be rich fall into temptation and a snare, and into many foolish and harmful lusts which drown men in destruction and perdition." If we hasten to be rich, we can be led astray. Proverbs 28:20 tells us, "A faithful man will abound with blessings, but he who hastens to be rich will not go unpunished."

Our emotions can be very intense and affect how we relate to others and direct the decisions we make. Yet by slowing down, thinking clearly, reassessing situations, recognizing that they are simply thoughts and that we can control them, we can decide on a different course of action.

We should practice self-control. Learning to control our thoughts and hence our emotions is a lifelong endeavor. The important thing to do is to cast all our cares and worries on the Lord (1 Pet. 5:7; Phil. 4:6) and to draw near to Him when we are anxious and stressed (James 4:8; Matt. 11:28).

Mapya was on the way back from preaching in eastern DRC with Ps. Mugisho. They met soldiers on the way back to Bukavu who stole their phones, money, and everything else they had and then beat them up. Some years later, Ps. Mugisho gave up because of the difficulties and hardship; he failed to overcome his negative experiences and subsequent negative feelings.

A Natural Perspective Leads to Negative Feelings

Our carnal feelings are often aroused by what we observe in this world. The psalmist Asaph lamented his sorry state when he saw the comfort of those who had forsaken the Lord: "For I was envious of the boastful, when I saw the prosperity of the wicked" (Ps. 73:3).

Overcome by Taking a Spiritual Perspective

Asaph went through a series of envious thoughts and struggles with regret until he sought the Lord and then came to a more spiritual viewpoint.

> When I thought how to understand this, it was too painful for me—until I went into the sanctuary of God; then I understood their end. (Ps. 73:16–17)

Speak the Correct Attitude to Our Souls

As we practice monitoring our emotional states, we can begin to speak correction to our hearts and rebuke our bad attitudes.

Why are you cast down, O my soul? And why are you disquieted within me? Hope in God, for I shall yet praise Him for the help of His countenance. (Ps. 42:5)

Here, David despaired about how bad he was feeling, but then he reproved himself and said, "Hey David. You need to hope in God! He will help you!"

We Can Change the Way We Think

Monitoring our emotional fluctuations and the reasoning behind them helps us nail down our flawed thinking processes as well. Just as Jesus rebuked the tempter with his negative thinking (Matt. 4; Luke 4), we can rebuke the temptation to give in to negative thoughts. As mentioned previously, we capture all our thoughts and bring them into subjection to the Spirit of God and the obedience of Christ; that leads us to a renewed mind (Eph. 4:23; Rom. 12:2), which is capable of focusing on the power of God when all seems lost according to our natural mindset.

> ... casting down arguments and every high thing that exalts itself against the knowledge of God, bringing every thought into captivity to the obedience of Christ. (2 Cor. 10:5)

> ... and be renewed in the spirit of your mind (Eph. 4:23)

> ... and do not be conformed to this world, but be transformed by the renewing of your mind, that you may prove what is that good and acceptable and perfect will of God. (Rom. 12:2)

Do not allow yourself to conform to this world's pattern of thinking. This world is anxious, stressed, fearful, doubting, unbelieving, sinful, confused, and riddled with selfish ambition, but we can live apart from such depression and rejection, amen! We can live with joy, love, and peace undergirded by self-control and patience. What a beautiful way to live!

Conclusion

Overcoming our feelings sounds impossible, but our feelings are a reflection of how we are thinking and responding to circumstances. These thoughts and responses can change. That is the power of the gospel! If that is true, we can change our feelings as well.

As we begin to be aware of our own feelings and reactions to different situations, we can track why we are feeling the way we do. As we expose our hidden thought processes, we can begin to redeem the way we think. As we do this, we redeem our minds, and our emotions and feelings will follow a more God-centered pattern.

God desires the best for us. He does not want us to lack any good thing. "The Lord is my shepherd, I shall not want!" (Ps. 23:1). Do we believe that as we follow the Lord, our lives will overflow with a good theme? "My heart overflows with a good theme" (Ps. 45:1). God does not want His people to have any lack especially in their emotional well-being.

How Do I Respond?

Jesus paid the price for all our blessings and for everything we will need in this life (2 Pet. 1:3; Eph. 1:3), so let us press on to know the Lord (Hos. 6:3) and follow His ways more and more (Mic. 4:2), amen! God doesn't want any of His people sick or diseased (1 Pet. 2:24).

We need to be loyal to Him (John 14:15) and trust and honor Him (Lev. 10:3). God provided water from a rock, manna from heaven, and quail from the sky for about 3 million people (Ex. 16:13), but He became upset with them when they complained about Him and didn't trust Him (Num. 11:1).

Chapter Summary

Let us consecrate ourselves to the Lord.
An incident can lead to a negative response that leads to negative thinking that gives rise to negative feelings.
Our feelings follow our thinking.
Do not be led by your feelings.
Practice self-control.

A natural perspective leads to negative feelings.
Overcome by taking a spiritual perspective.
Speak the correct attitude to your soul.
We can change the way we think.

Reference

Grant Van Boeschoten. 2008. "Setting Up Your Life To Succeed In The Eyes Of God," https://www.sermoncentral.com/sermons/setting-up-your-life-to-succeed-in-the-eyes-of-god-grant-van-boeschoten-sermon-on-growth-in-christ-118530.

EPILOGUE

For this reason, when I could no longer endure it, **I sent
to know your faith**, lest by some means the tempter
had tempted you, and our labor might be in vain.

—1 Thessalonians 3:5

The life and journey of faith is the most exciting way we can live. It is a connection with our heavenly Father that is constant and alive. It is the belief that He is with us and will never leave us or forsake us no matter what happens to us (Dan. 3:17–18). By faith, we know that God will bring about His purposes for our lives and that our lives can have eternal fruit and influence people for eternity.

The apostle Paul wrote about the "spirit of faith."

> And since we have the same spirit of faith, according to
> what is written, **"I believed and therefore I spoke,"** we
> also believe and therefore speak. (2 Cor 4:13)

We live and speak by faith ("The just shall live by his faith," Hab. 2:4). We can get to this place where everything we do is consecrated to God each day and we walk by faith (without doubting) each day!

Remember that in regard to the spiritual realm, our thoughts are just as important as our words. Please be careful about your thoughts because what you think in your heart is what you will eventually believe (Prov. 4:23, 23:7) because faith is in the heart.

Jesus exhorted us, "For out of the abundance of the heart the mouth speaks" (Matt. 12:34; Luke 6:45), so what we meditate on in our hearts is so crucial to our spiritual lives and the development of our faith.

This walk of faith opens the door for complete trust in God's power and providence in our lives and for a supernatural peace to guard our hearts and minds (Isa. 26:3; Phil. 4:7; Col. 3:15). Wonderful are the promises of the Lord, amen!

ACKNOWLEDGMENTS

For in it (the Gospel of Christ) the righteousness of God is revealed
from faith to faith; as it is written, "The just shall live by faith."

—Romans 1:17

I thank my wife, Helen, who has been fully supportive of and completely engaged in our ministry in church planting here in Adelaide and Perth and overseas in India and Africa. She has been an exceptional blessing and fellow warrior.

I also must thank HIM and its leadership (Ps. Wilson and Ps. Simon) without whom we would never have had the faith or the vision to believe that we could ever plant a church. We thank God for our apostolic leaders and the biblical vision imparted to us.

Our church family in Adelaide has been a great blessing and support in building the church with us; we love them as our own family and thank God for our colaborers.

Ps. Andrew Evans, Ps. Mapya, Ps. Ravi, Ps. Jackson, Ps Sonny and Ps Benny in particular have imparted many spiritual jewels into our lives as we have traveled to their countries to minister and have been enriched by the Lord in return. We are so grateful to have our spiritual frontiers broadened and widened by these relationships and experiences.

Printed in the United States
by Baker & Taylor Publisher Services